# SUMMONING THE GODS:
## *Sandpainting in the Native American Southwest*

by Ronald McCoy

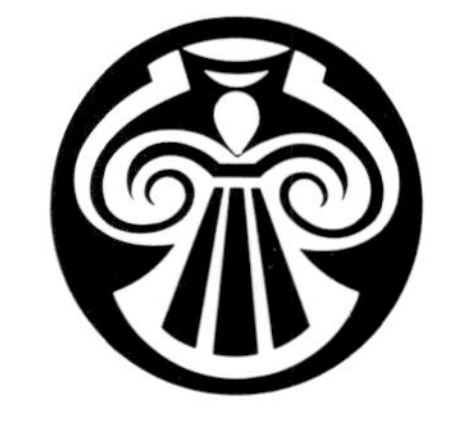

Museum of Northern Arizona

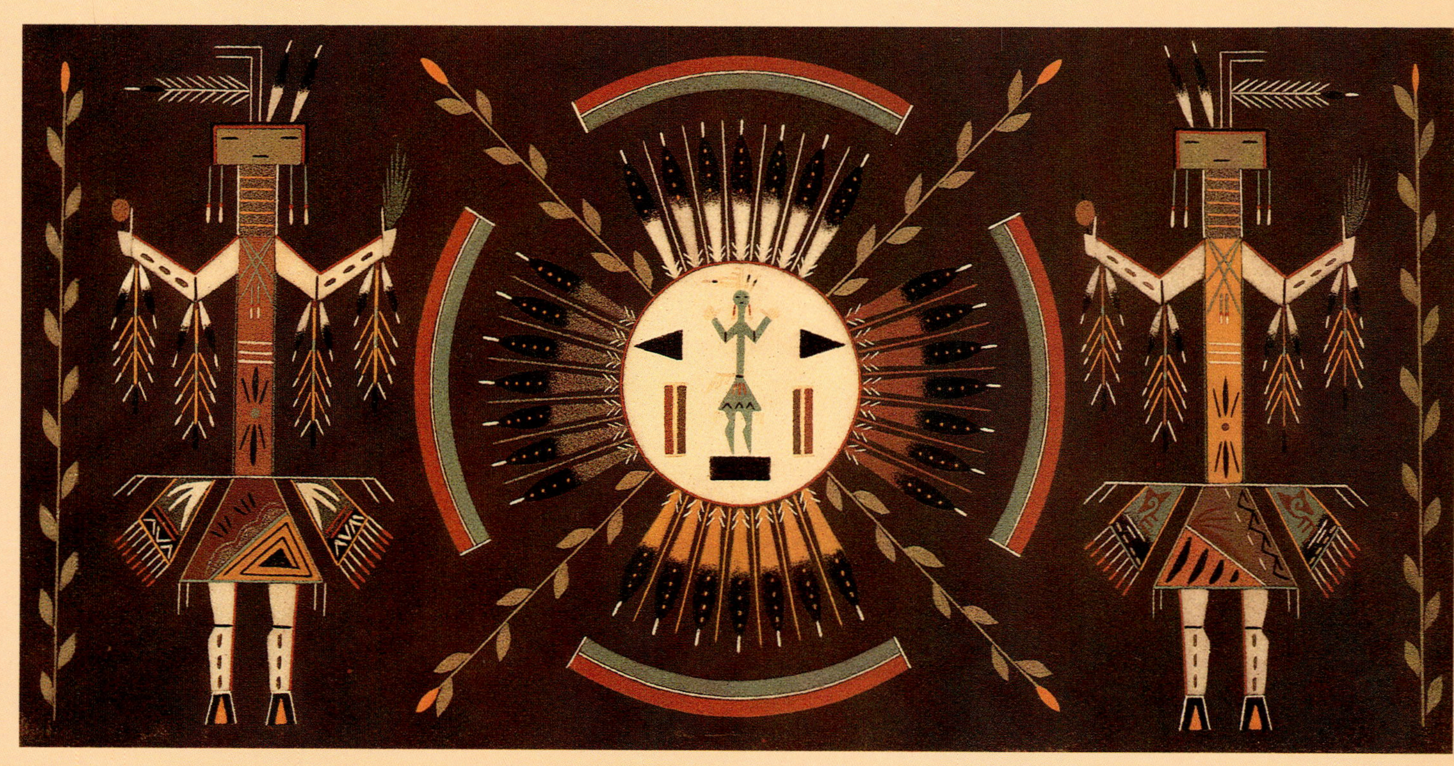

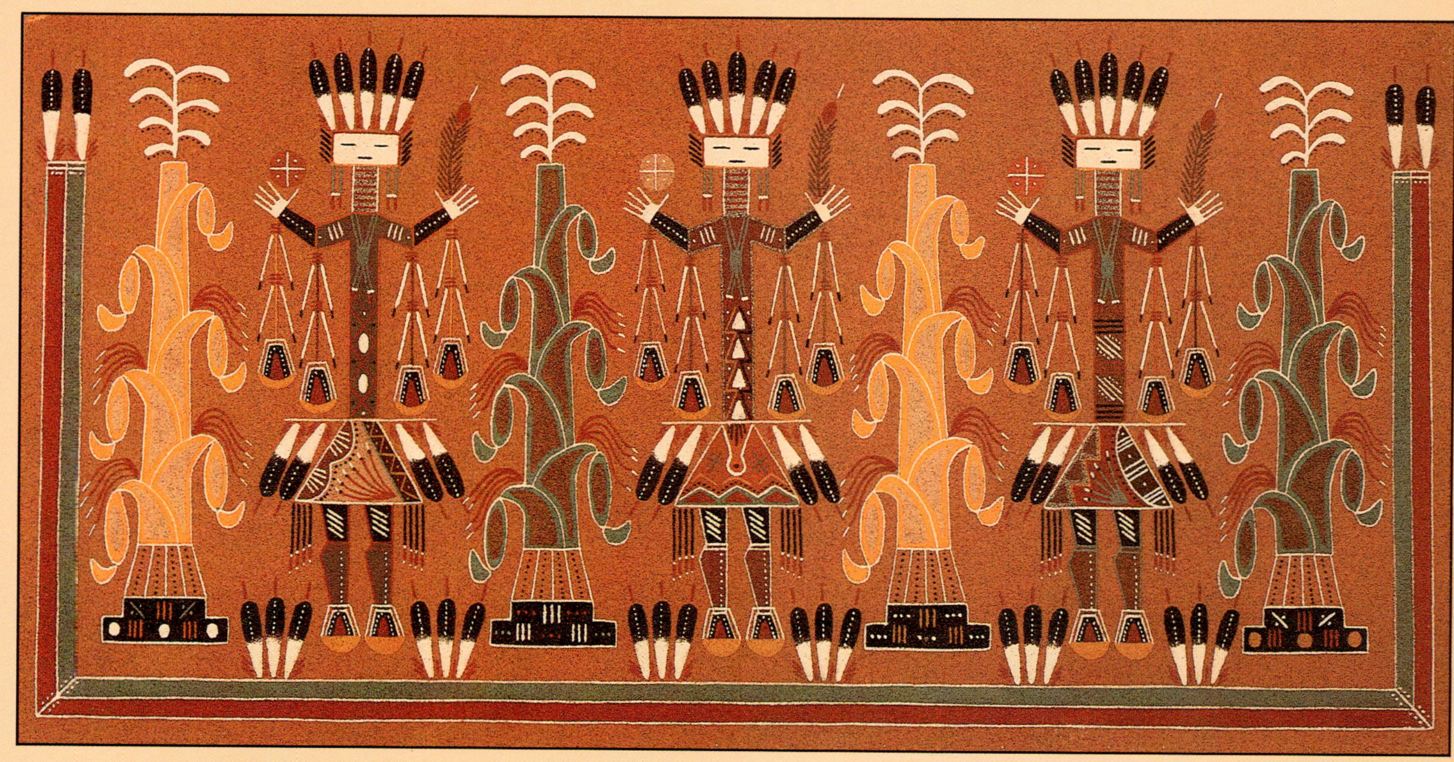

# Sandpaintings as Sacred Art and Symbolic Language

In all times, places, and cultures, people have sought to understand the world in which they live. Private yearnings, prayers in cathedrals, incantations at mountaintop shrines, rites of passage, choruses of hope—all seek the same goal: a relationship with the primal forces of the universe through which people hope to prolong, enhance, or otherwise favorably affect their lives.

For traditional Native Americans, the object of attention in matters spiritual is a variegated tapestry of spirits, or, more loosely, a pantheon of the gods. These inspiring forces of mysterious power are summoned through rites and rituals as numerous and diverse as humankind itself. Among these pleas for divine intervention is the sandpainting of the Native American Southwest, surely one of the most intriguing methods for summoning the gods.

The underlying principle of this sacred art dictates that pigments obtained from charcoal, clays, minerals, and plants of Mother Earth can be arranged to create transitory designs of religious significance. These designs are nothing less than prayers, requests for the attention of powerful spirits. Through the intercession of a religious specialist, a medicine man, the supernaturals respond to the lure of the sandpainting by temporarily inhabiting it. In this way, an image created by humans becomes, for a time, the dwelling place of gods. These spirits may aid in bringing rain to a thirsty earth and parched crops or bestow blessings upon people by alleviating their mental and physical ills.

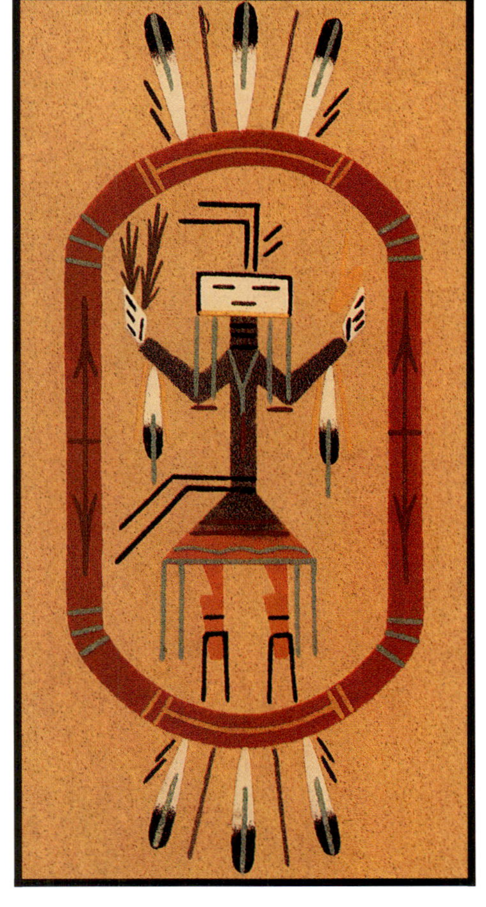

Sandpainting, or drypainting*, is a fairly widespread tradition in the Native American Southwest. This sacred art attains its dramatic and inspiring apotheosis among the Navajos of the Four Corners country, where the borders of Arizona, Utah, Colorado, and New Mexico meet.

*"Drypainting" is a more precise description for this art since sand usually serves only as a background, not a medium. Nevertheless, "sandpainting" still is the most commonly used and widely recognized name.

Opposite, Top: "Sun and Eagle with Yei" by Nelson Lewis
MNA Gift Shop. Photograph by Gene Balzer
Opposite, Bottom: Sandpainting by Rosabelle Ben
MNA Gift Shop. Photograph by Gene Balzer
Above: "Yei with Guardian Circle and Feathers" by W & E Yazzie
MNA Gift Shop. Photograph by Gene Balzer

# GIFTS FROM THE GODS

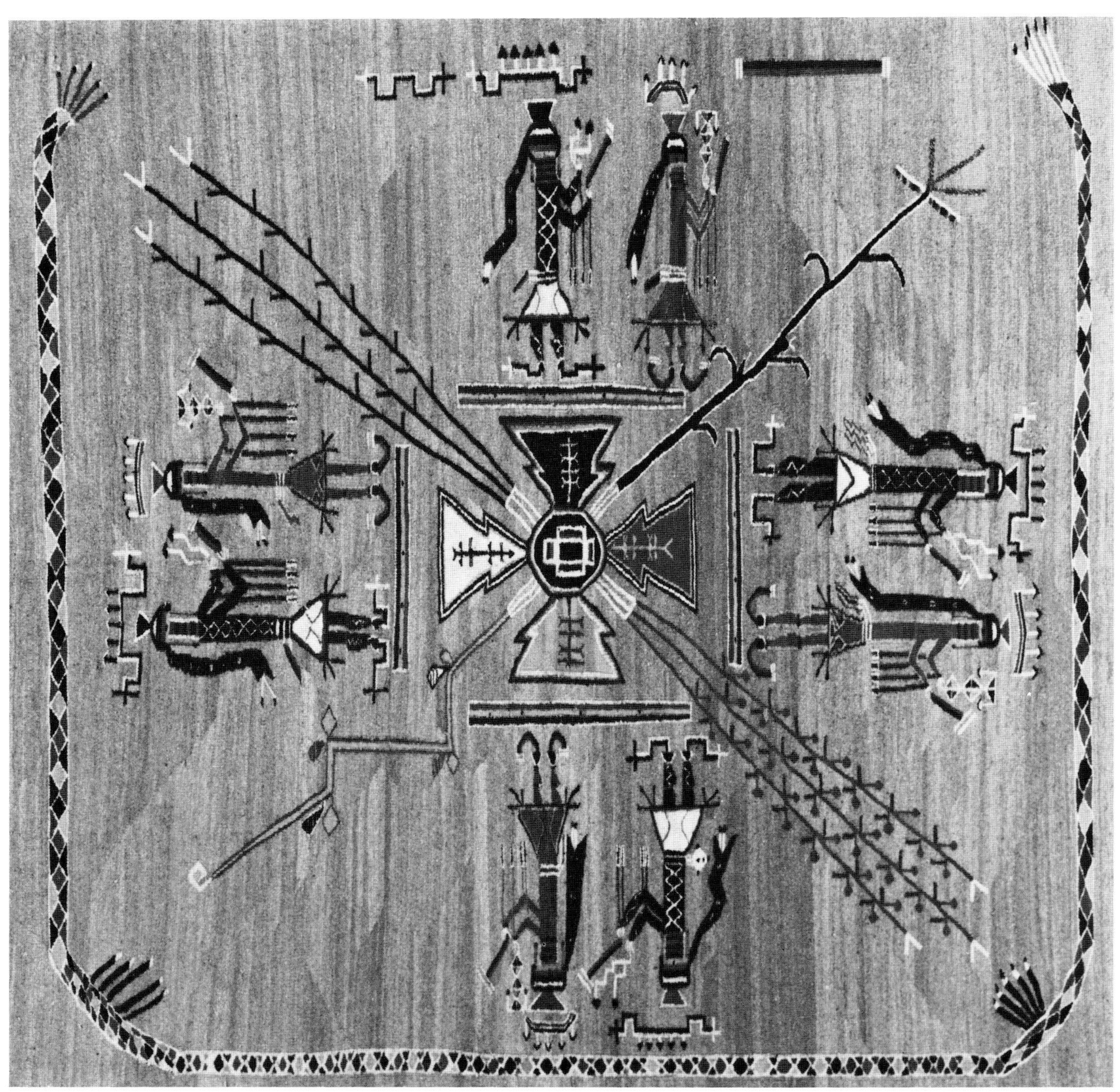

Navajo Klah Sandpainting Rug. Handspun, 67" x 72",
Gladwin Collection, 1925-1935. Photograph by Gene Balzer

Navajos, members of the largest Indian tribe in North America, inhabit an eighteen million-acre reservation in the Four Corners country. This reservation overlaps into southeastern Utah but is located primarily in Arizona and New Mexico. The ancestral home held dear by the Navajos is a 30,000 square-mile tribal heartland along the Upper San Juan River known as Dinetah, often freely translated as Navajoland, a term now used for the whole reservation.

Most archaeologists and anthropologists believe Navajo hunters and gatherers arrived in Dinetah between A.D. 1000 and 1525, and certainly they were well entrenched by the early 17th century. The Navajos cleave to a different view, one intimately connected with their drypainting practices.

In the beginning, so weavers of tales from the time of Navajo legends say, were the Holy People—Snake People, Spider Woman, Corn People, First Man and First Woman, and many, many others. They lived in worlds below this one and were guided by First Man in ascending to the world in which we Earth Surface People now live.

The Holy People kept permanent paintings of sacred designs on spiders' webs, sheets of sky, clouds, fog, fabric, and buckskin. They bestowed the right to make copies of these paintings upon protagonists in the origin stories, which recount ceremonies in which sandpaintings were first created. An account of one of the Holy People, Monster Slayer, transferring drypainting images to a mythological hero has been preserved:

> Next, four sheets of sky were brought forth. A white sheet was spread on the floor in the east; a blue sheet in the south; a yellow sheet in the west and a dark sheet in the north. On each of these sheets was painted a picture, which the Navajo was told to study with care and remember. When he had done this they rolled up again the sheets of sky and Nayenezgani [Monster Slayer] said: 'Such pictures you must teach your people to draw. They cannot do this on sheets of sky as we do; but they can grind to powder stones of various colors and draw their pictures on sand.' (Washington Matthews, *The Night Chant*, 1902)

The Navajos began to create copies of the gods' paintings in sacred rituals, which most frequently are conducted at night. These copies of the pictures kept by the Holy People assume the form of sandpaintings depicting anthropomorphic supernaturals, the four sacred plants (corn, beans, squash, and tobacco), clouds, animals, and numerous other objects. Usually, drypaintings are made inside a Navajo home, an eight-sided, cribbed-log dwelling called a hogan. The paintings often are laid out on a one-to-three-inch-thick bed of fresh sand that has been smoothed with a wooden weaving batten, though sometimes a buckskin or cloth serves as a surface.

Pigments used for painting traditionally are placed in bark dishes. These days, however, plastic plates and pieces of cardboard often suffice. Color sources include pulverized gypsum (white), yellow ochre, red sandstone, charcoal, and a mixture of charcoal and gypsum (blue). Brown can be obtained by mixing red and black, while red and white yield pink. In addition, Navajo sandpainters also rely on pollen, cornmeal, and crushed flower petals.

The principal drypainting colors—white, blue, yellow, and black—convey symbolic meaning and are linked with the Four Sacred Mountains marking the boundaries of Dinetah, the traditional tribal universe: White Shell Peak in the east is associated with the dawn; Blue Turquoise Mountain to the south signals the sky; Yellow Abalone Shell Mountain off in the west connotes twilight; and darkness belongs to Black Coal Mountain on the northern periphery.

The Navajo term for sandpainting is ′iikááh, "place where the gods come and go." It is an appropriate name since the designs are employed in ceremonies designed to summon supernatural forces. Navajos most often use sandpainting in curing rituals that are conducted by an hatáálii, a "Singer" or medicine man. A patient troubled by physical or mental ills sits on the painting facing east toward the

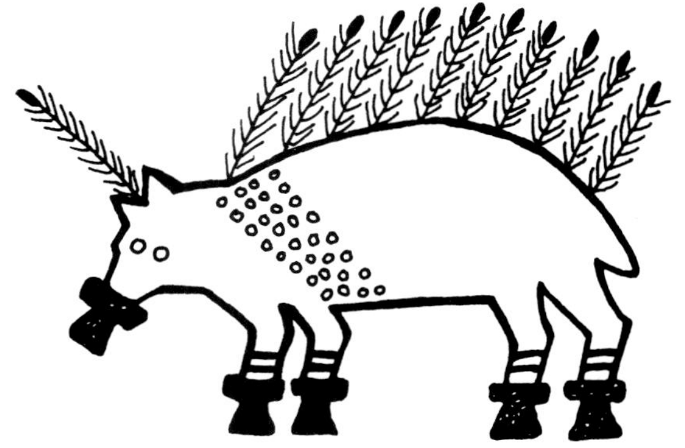

Bear constellation

hogan's darkened doorway. The Holy People who are being summoned will arrive from this direction and infuse the sandpainting with their healing power. In this way, the evil causing the physical or mental hurt is dispelled, and future threats from malevolent forces are blunted.

Small sandpaintings (those one or two feet across) can be made by a couple of men in an hour or so. On the other end of the spectrum, mammoth creations twenty feet wide or more require the labor of fifteen men for most of a day. Since greatness of size and the repetition of sacred symbols are considered most effective, it is not surprising that drypaintings average about six to eight feet across.

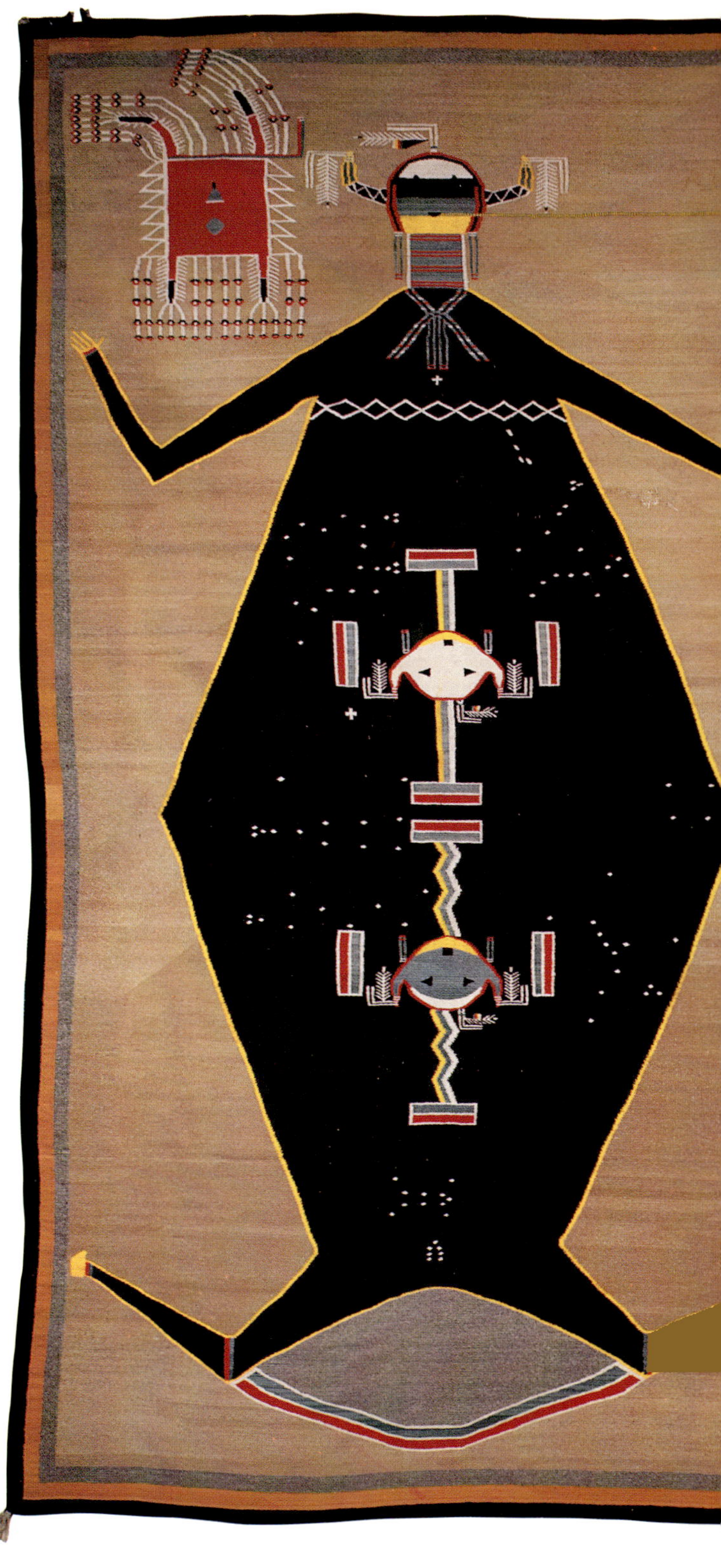

Navajo Sandpainting Rug. Made by Atlnabah. Photograph from MNA collections

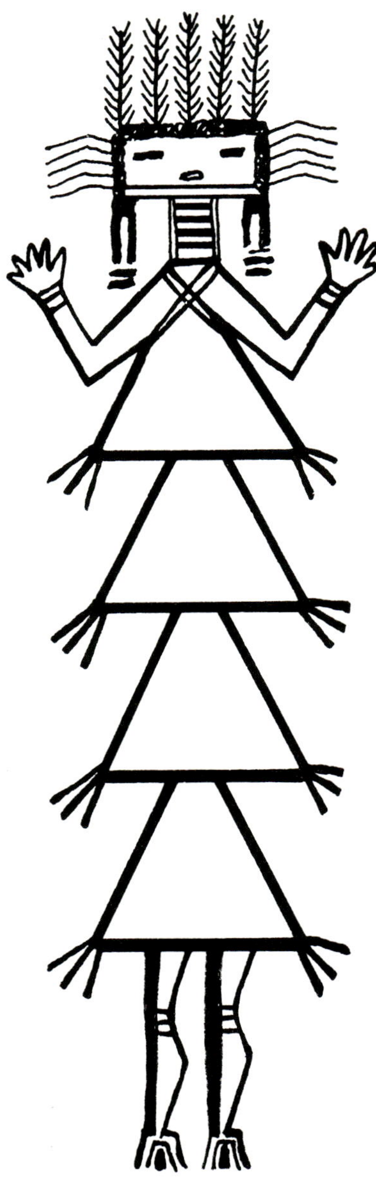

Mountain god wearing four blankets of fire

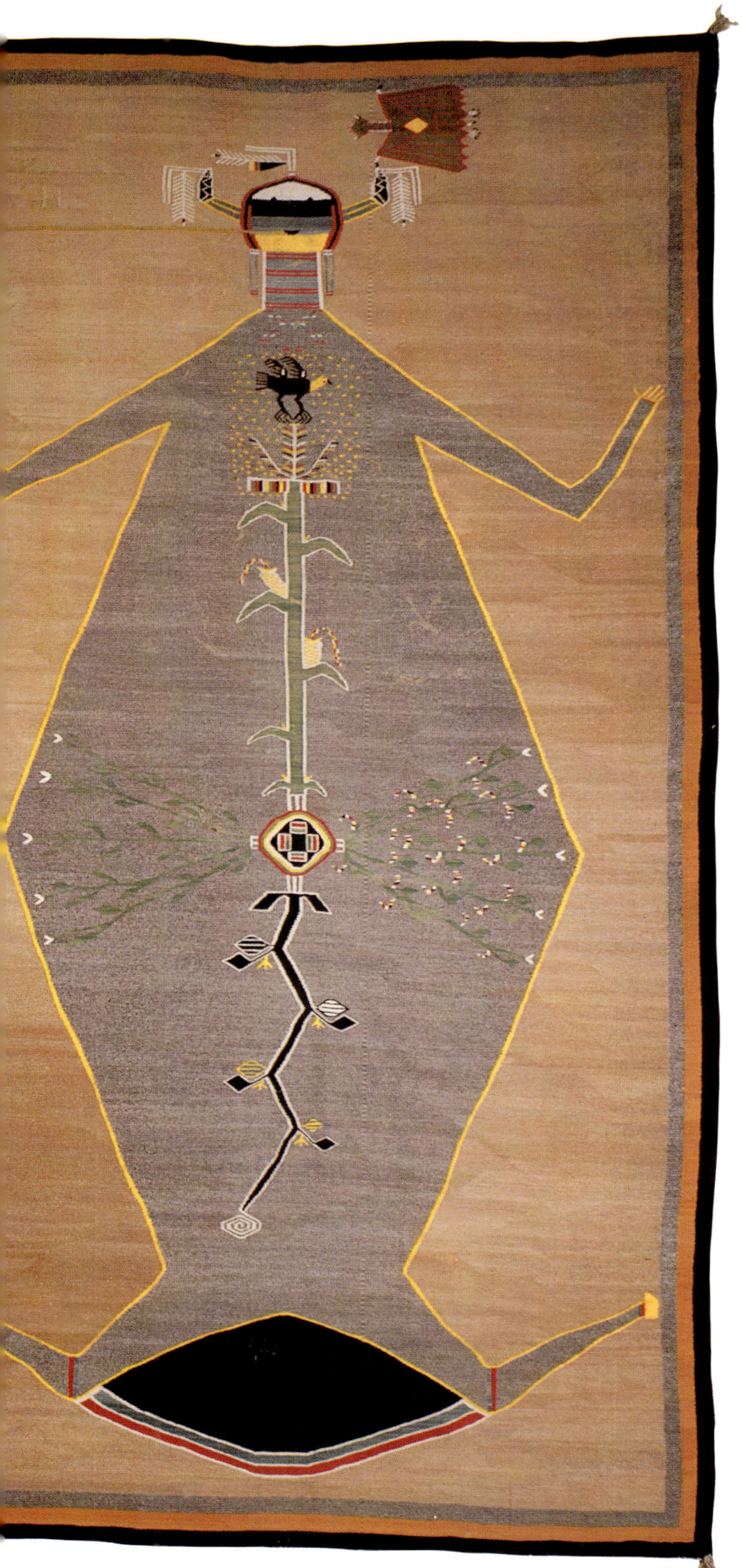

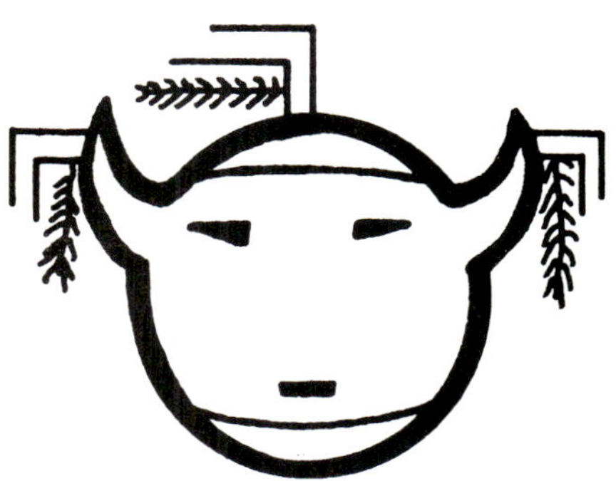

Sun or moon symbol

Sandpaintings are made under the Singer's direction by men (though women may help on occasion) who let the pigment trickle between their thumb and flexed forefinger. For practical reasons, painters work outward from the center of the picture. For religious reasons, a ritualistic "sunwise" pattern is followed, with work beginning in the east, thence south, west, north, and finally finishing in the east.

Sandpaintings are laid out along three general design patterns: linear, radial, and extended-center. Linear paintings depict figures arranged in one or more lines suspended over a groundbar. Radial sandpaintings feature images arranged in an illusory rotating, or whirling, pattern around a center point. Those created within an extended-center pattern display a central motif so enlarged as to dominate the composition. In most cases, these compositions are surrounded by a protective garland representing a spiritual guardian, such as a rainbow, lightning, snakes, even sunflowers. Additional guardians may appear at a painting's eastern opening. These guardians, whatever form they assume, all serve to protect the magical realm encapsulated within the sandpainting.

Upon completion of the drypainting the patient receives the medicine man's ministerings, including the singing of such poetically moving prayers as this:

In the house of long life, there I wander.
In the house of happiness, there I wander.
Beauty before me, with it I wander.
Beauty behind me, with it I wander.
Beauty below me, with it I wander.
Beauty above me, with it I wander.
Beauty all around me, with it I wander.
In old age traveling, with it I wander.
I am on the beautiful trail, with it I wander.
(Washington Matthews, "Navaho Myths, Prayers and Songs", 1907)

The Singer's repetoire also provides chanted formulas for divine manifestations as this one:

Oh, Male God!
With your moccasins of dark cloud,
come to us.
With your leggings of dark cloud,
come to us.
With your shirt of dark cloud,
come to us.
With your head-dress of dark cloud,
come to us.
With your mind enveloped in dark cloud,
come to us.
With the dark thunder above you,
come to us soaring.
With the shaped cloud at your feet,
come to us soaring.
With the far darkness made of the dark cloud
over your head,
come to us soaring.
With the far darkness made of the he-rain over
your head,
come to us soaring.
With the far darkness made of the dark mist over
your head,
come to us soaring.
With the far darkness made of the she-rain over
your head,
come to us soaring.
With the zigzag lightning flung out on high over
your head,
come to us soaring.
With the rainbow hanging high over your head,
come to us soaring.
With the far darkness made of the dark cloud on
the ends of your wings,
come to us soaring.
With the far darkness made of the he-rain on the
ends of your wings,
come to us soaring.
With the far darkness made of the dark mist on
the ends of your wings,
come to us soaring.
With the far darkness made of the she-rain on
the ends of your wings,
come to us soaring.
With the zigzag lightning flung out on high on
the ends of your wings,
come to us soaring.
With the rainbow hanging high on the ends of
your wings,
come to us soaring.
With the near darkness made of the dark cloud, of
the he-rain, of the dark mist, and of the she-rain,
come to us.
With the darkness on the earth,
come to us. (Washington Matthews, *The Night
Chant*, 1902 )

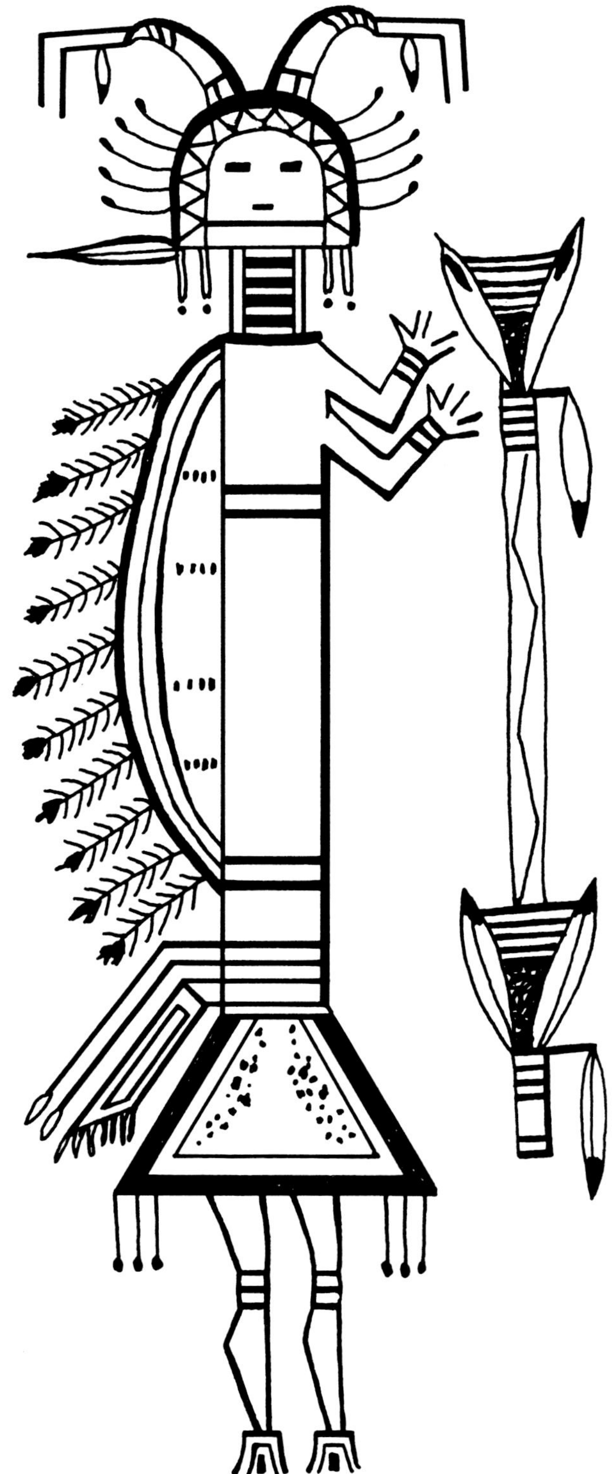

Beganaskiddy, carrier of seeds, with his ceremonial cane and horns of power

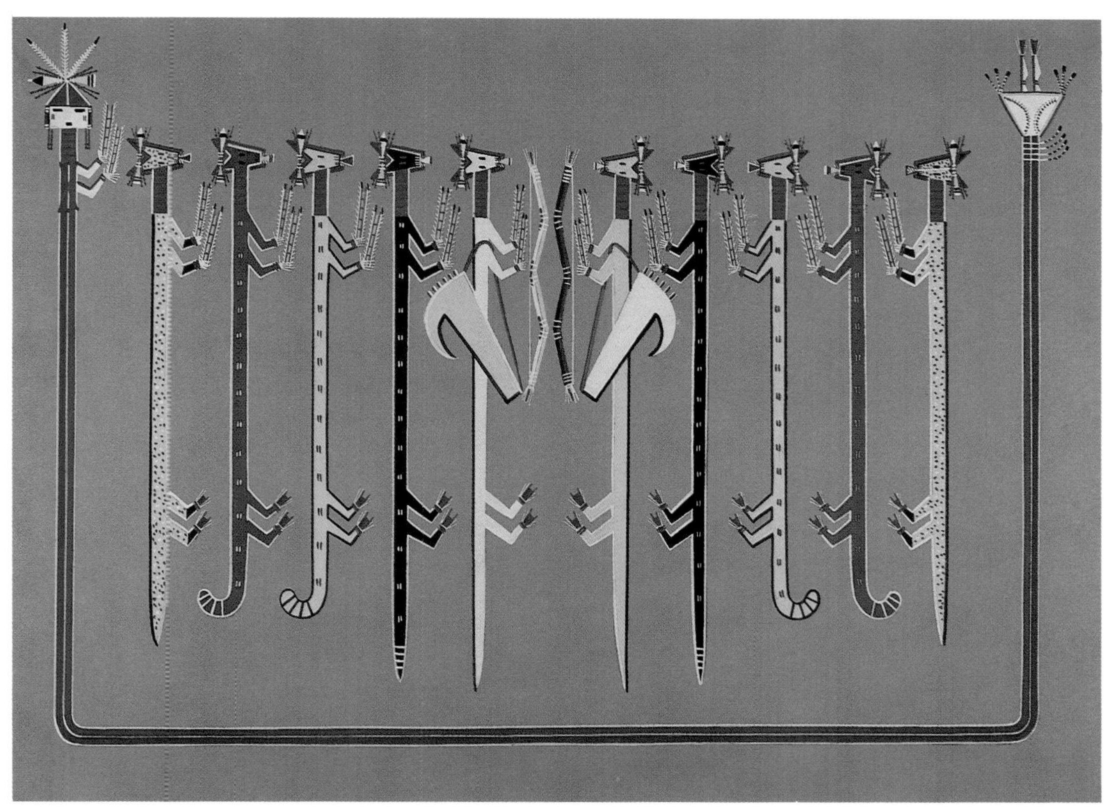

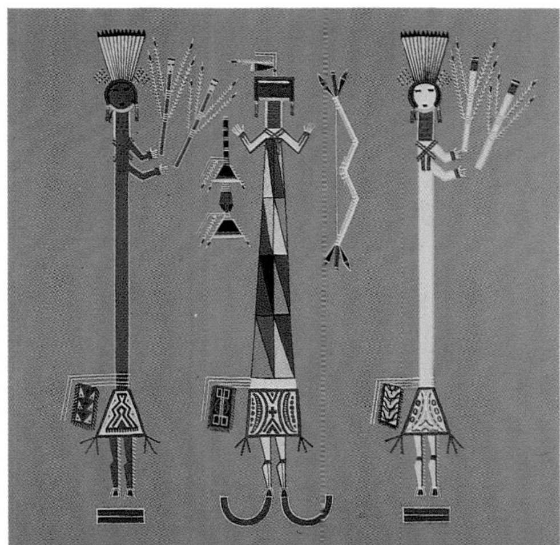

Top: "The Exchange of Quivers" by Fred Geary. Photograph by Gene Balzer
Left: Shooting Chant: Prayer Group. "Prayer Painting of Ted-de-gini" by Fred Geary. Photograph by Gene Balzer
Bottom: "The Final Ascension of Scavenger Attended by Lightnings (Snakes)" by Fred Geary. Photograph by Gene Balzer

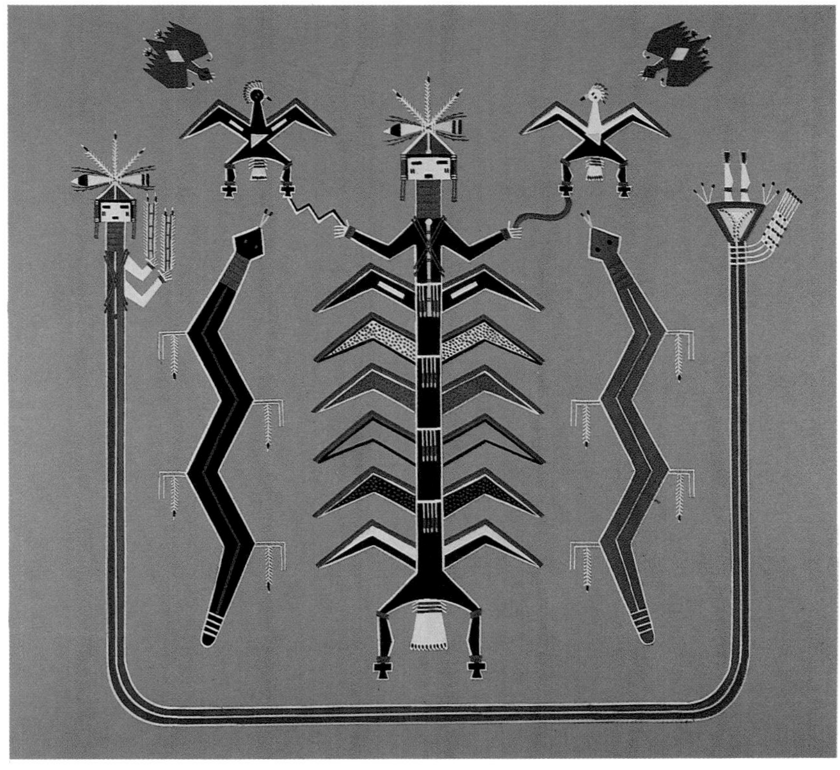

As the ceremony approaches its climax, the Singer removes objects from his medicine bundle, which contains such ritual paraphernalia as gourd or hide rattles and the like. He touches them to the body parts of Holy People in the painting, then to his own corresponding parts, and, finally, to those of the patient. When the ritual is concluded, the drypainting is destroyed by the Singer in the reverse order of its creation and literally swept away.

Destruction of the drypainting is essential, for the Holy People are at once revered and feared. The failure to make a drypainting anew each time a design is used, for example, may bring blindness or death to the transgressor. But there is respect as well as fear in this tradition. If any one message is clearly conveyed in Navajo myths, it is this: the universe is a wondrous place, filled with Holy People of great beauty, mystery, and danger.

At its most fundamental level, sandpainting is a strategy for dealing with forces considerably more powerful and infinitely more complex than anything ordinary mortals are capable of understanding. According to traditional Navajo belief, the universe is affected by that which is "good," or under control, and that which is "evil," or out of control. Between these two extremes lies hózhó, an amalgamation of such concepts as "balanced," "pleasant," "blessed," "holy," and "beautiful."

Hózhó bridges the forces of opposition and creates balance. But this balance is difficult to maintain because the universe and its Holy People—each supernatural, every rock, plant, tree, mountain, animal, person, star, and planet—are not only alive but easily offended. A person who arouses the ire of any of these forces, knowingly or otherwise, creates disorder and risks mental anguish, physical torment, even death.

The list of taboos—practices and behaviors prohibited lest they disrupt balance—is extensive. Killing a bear, for example, may cause arthritis. Nasal problems often are associated with squirrels, while eating a turkey might lead to itching or pimples. And mountain sheep are linked to both deafness and disorders of the eye. Other problems of even greater seriousness arise from the malevolent practices of witches, the bane of Navajo existence. Witches commonly are believed to make sandpaintings for their own twisted rituals. These drypaintings, made of colored ash, are sometimes said to depict the evil-doers' intended victims.

Reintroducing balance requires someone to manipulate the universe's opposing, interrelated forces by trafficking with the supernatural. This calls for the sort of power that comes from knowledge of a dangerous and very special kind. This knowledge is acquired by those who apprentice themselves to medicine men and eventually become Singers. By contacting the elemental forces of the cosmos through chanting ceremonies, Singers alleviate suffering and ensure that a patient will not be troubled again by the effects of having come into contact with dangerous forces. Hózhó is then reinstituted.

The core of Navajo religion is the ceremony Blessingway, which conveys hózhó to childbirth, a new home, marriage, livestock, crops, and so on. In Blessingway small drypaintings made from pollen, flower petals, and crushed minerals are sometimes made on buckskin or cloth. Navajo religion also includes "chantways"—named after the forces with which they deal, such as Red Antway and Coyoteway. It is in these that sandpaintings abound. In Shootingway, for example, medicine men may select from an array of about a hundred different drypainting designs.

Each chantway is connected to an origin myth. For example, Hailway is associated with a series of episodes involving Rain Boy, a gambler who lost all of his family's possessions. Warned by Bat Woman of the beating his comrades intended to administer to him, Rain Boy fled his home and commenced the wanderings commemorated by the Hailway chants. Early on in his odyssey, he came to a hogan within which dwelled a beautiful woman. But her husband, Winter Thunder, became jealous and shattered Rain Boy's body with hail. Many Holy People gathered together and restored Rain Boy. Later, after suffering defeat at the hands of Rain Boy's Holy People allies, Winter Thunder conducted a healing ceremony for his former enemy. More adventures followed, and by the time Rain Boy returned to his own people, he was semi-divine. He taught the ceremonies he learned to his older brother and departed, to live forever with the Holy People.

A number of chantway ceremonies have "male" and "female" branches, perhaps in deference to the sex of the mythical hero. Female Mountainway, for example, includes accounts of a Navajo girl attempting to escape from Bear Man. Some chantway rituals are extinct, others nearly so. Those most frequently performed today are Mountainway, Nightway, Navajo Windway, Shootingway, Chiricahua Windway, Hand-tremblingway, and Flintway.

Particular physical and mental disorders require particular chantways. Shootingway, for instance, is the remedy prescribed by a medicine man who diagnoses a patient's respiratory or gastrointestinal problems as emanating from difficulties associated with thunder, lightning, and snakes.

Singers perform chantways in two-, five-, and nine-night variations that contain two principal parts. The first task is purification and exorcism of evil. This is followed by the attraction of supernatural powers to reinstitute balance. It is in the second part of chantway ritual, the summoning of the gods, that drypaintings are made.

The five hundred or so types of Navajo sandpaintings that have been recorded (possibly a like number have not been documented) contain a rich symbolic language. This holy vocabulary of sacred designs eloquently conveys esoteric messages to mortals and Holy People alike. Yet far more is involved than simply imparting stories or depicting divinities. The paintings' symbols, sources of power in a temporary abode of holiness, must be treated with respect. One does not, for example, step into or walk across a completed sandpainting but around it in the ritually prescribed clockwise direction.

The First Family—Holy Man and Holy Woman, Holy Boy and Holy Girl—frequently appear in drypaintings. Other supernaturals, such as the Ye'i (Failed to Speak People), Earth and Sky, Sun and Moon, and Thunders and Winds, figure prominently—as do a host of Animal People and Plant People. Certain types of supernaturals are confined only to sandpaintings of particular chantways. One of these is Changing Woman.

Changing Woman created the first Navajos, and she alone among Holy People always does good things for the tribe. It was Changing Woman who gave the tribe the Blessingway rituals that nourish all other Navajo belief. Impregnated by rays of Sun, she bore twin sons, Monster Slayer and Born for Water. When these Hero Twins set out in search of their father, Sun attempted to freeze them. But Otter and Beaver loaned the Twins their skins for protection. For this reason, these animals often are depicted as guardians. Illustrations of Changing Woman are featured only in the Blessingway rituals.

The dramatic Night Sky composition is found only in Hailway paintings. Buffalo People appear in connection with the sandpaintings of Shootingway, Coyote People in those used for Coyoteway, Wind People in Navajo Windway depictions, and Ant People in Red Antway illustrations—and nowhere else. But other figures, such as the Hero Twins, Corn

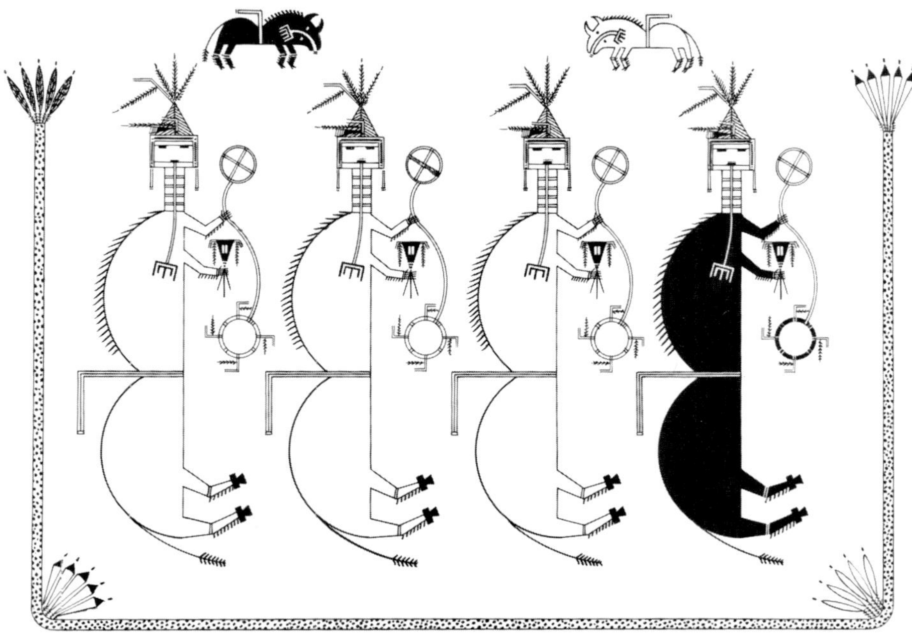

"The Buffalo at Red Water" by Fred Geary. Photograph by Gene Balzer

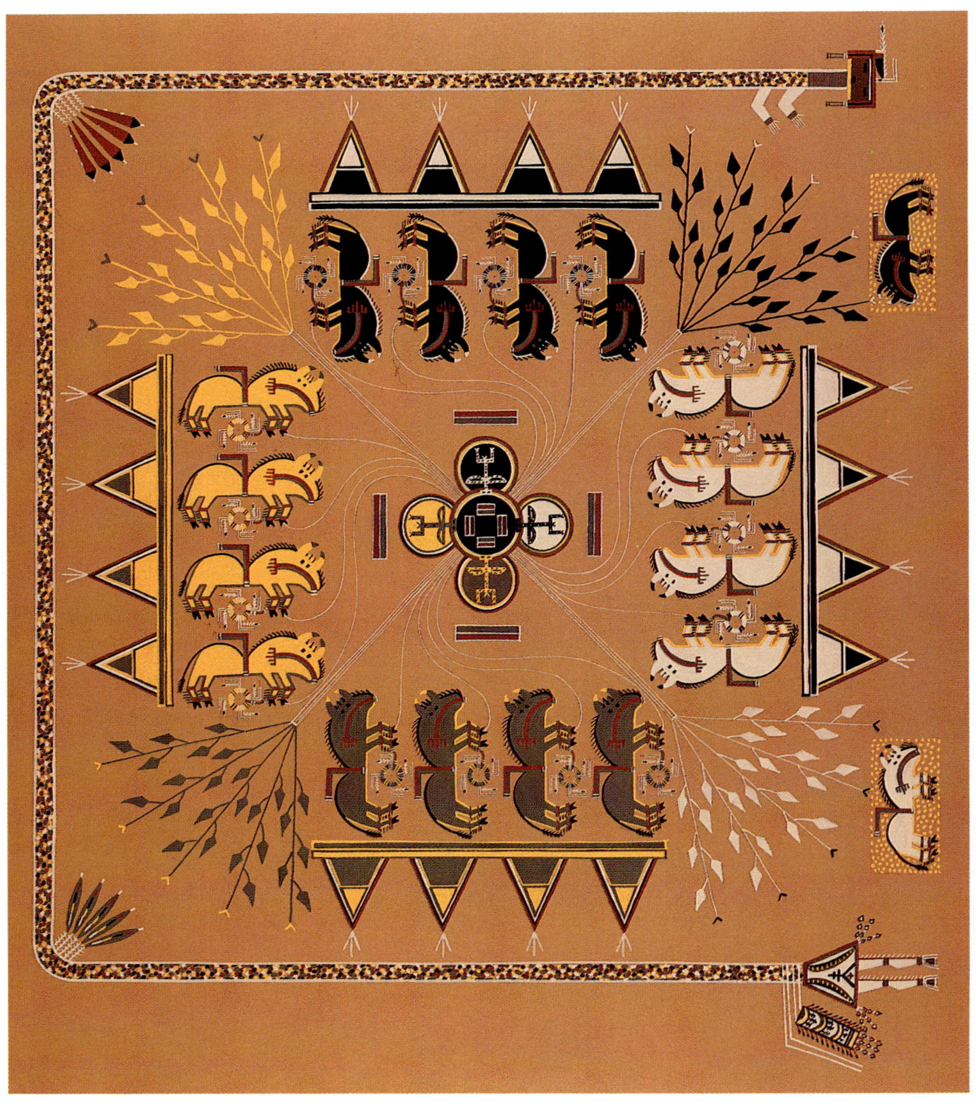

Shooting Chant: Buffalo Group by Fred Geary. Photograph by Gene Balzer

People, Big Fly, the Emergence Place where First Man brought Holy People into this world, as well as a host of other images are found in the drypaintings of various chants. Sun and Moon, for example, are found in the sandpaintings of no less than nine different chantways.

The theory underlying the creation of Navajo sandpaintings is deceptively simple. Each drypainting serves as a lure, calling upon Holy People to view their own images. Once summoned, treated with respect, and propitiated in ways known to the medicine man, Holy People are obliged to act with a spirit of reciprocity. Pleased by the Singer's work, mindful of reverence in the hogan, and heeding prayers, Holy People do their part by restoring balance, or hózhó, to the patient. Although this explanation of sandpainting's purpose seems reasonably plain enough, there is much subtlety at work in the process.

By following the medicine man's directions, crossing into the holy realm, and sitting on the sandpainting, the patient becomes a part of the painting, thereby achieving temporary union with the supernatural. This association is dramatized by the medicine man's application of pigment from figures in the painting to matching parts of the patient's body. The sequence through which power and blessings are acquired and subsequently transferred follows this continuum: from the original source (the Holy People), to the sacred vehicle (the sandpainting), into the hands of the schooled manipulator of supernatural forces (the Singer), and, finally, to the ultimate beneficiary (the patient).

Just as the patient absorbs blessings from the painting, so the patient, in turn, is absorbed by this sacred creation. Anthropologist Gladys Reichard, a keen and especially gifted student of Navajo religion, described this process of exchanging evil for good as a kind of "spiritual osmosis."

But how does the cure work? Donald Sandner, a clinical psychiatrist who began working on the Navajo reservation in 1968, recalls a medicine man suggesting one answer to this question. "If the patient really has confidence in me, then he gets cured," the Singer told Sandner. "If he has no confidence, then that is his problem." In other words, as Sandner puts it, "the patient shares the responsibility for his cure." As a psychiatrist, Sandner found the chantways fascinating. His studies led him to the conclusion that one of the critical elements in sandpainting ritual involves the patient's confession to the Singer of taboo violation. This is followed by the Singer providing absolution, the dispersal of evil, and the restoration of balance. As for the sandpaintings themselves, these are symbols which Sandner perceives as "intrapsychic" agents. The patient is immersed in a situation calling for repeated chanting and intense concentration upon symbols. Thus, the curative pattern is repeated "over and over again, until the connection is made and the same symbolic pattern 'lights up' in the patient's psyche....Then, by the grace of the gods, the transformation may occur, and if the symbol that impresses itself upon the receptive psyche is potent enough, the effects could be permanent." Sandner's study of sandpainting also led him to conclude that the Navajos "have constructed an edifice of symbolism that can take its place among the great healing systems of the world."

However beneficial a sandpainting may be, this window on the supernatural cannot remain open forever. If Holy People come in response to the painting's summons and find no ritual and no respect, they will become angry. When the ire of Holy People is aroused, hózhó is once again disturbed, and the balance the medicine man infuses into the world through drypainting vanishes. This is why curing rituals are performed immediately upon the sandpainting's completion. It also is why a Singer brushes the sandpainting into oblivion—in reverse order from its creation—at the ceremony's conclusion. Then, the sand is carried outside in sacks and deposited north of the hogan often beside the nearest lightning-struck tree. There it remains, a barrier to the return of exorcised evil.

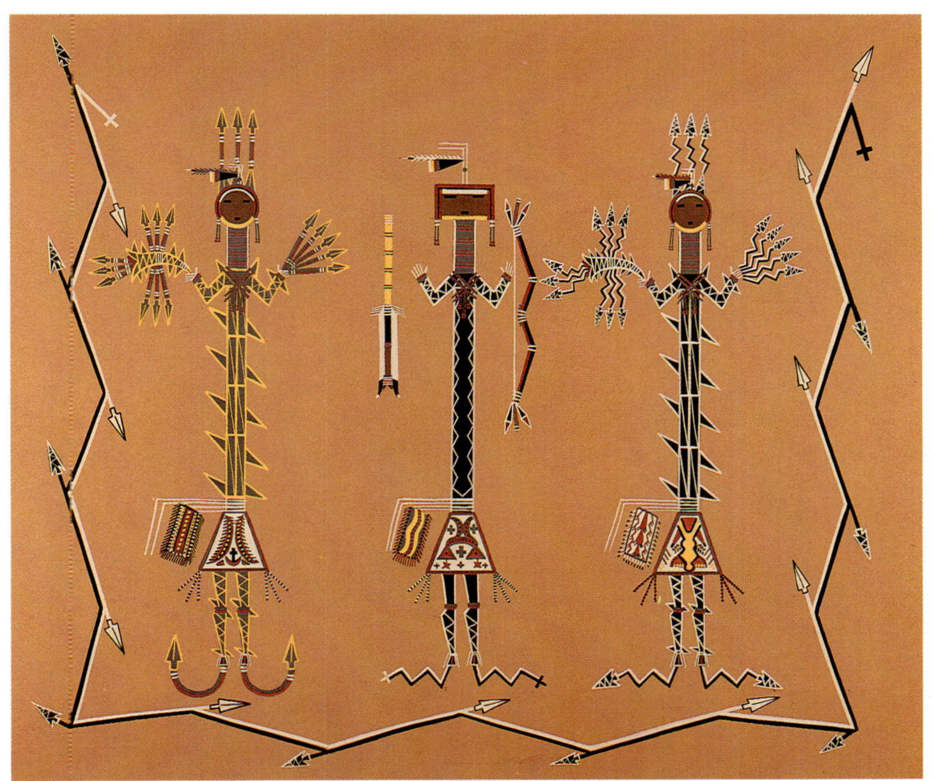

Shooting Chant: Prayer Group by Fred Geary. Photograph by Gene Balzer

# Other Southwestern Drypainting

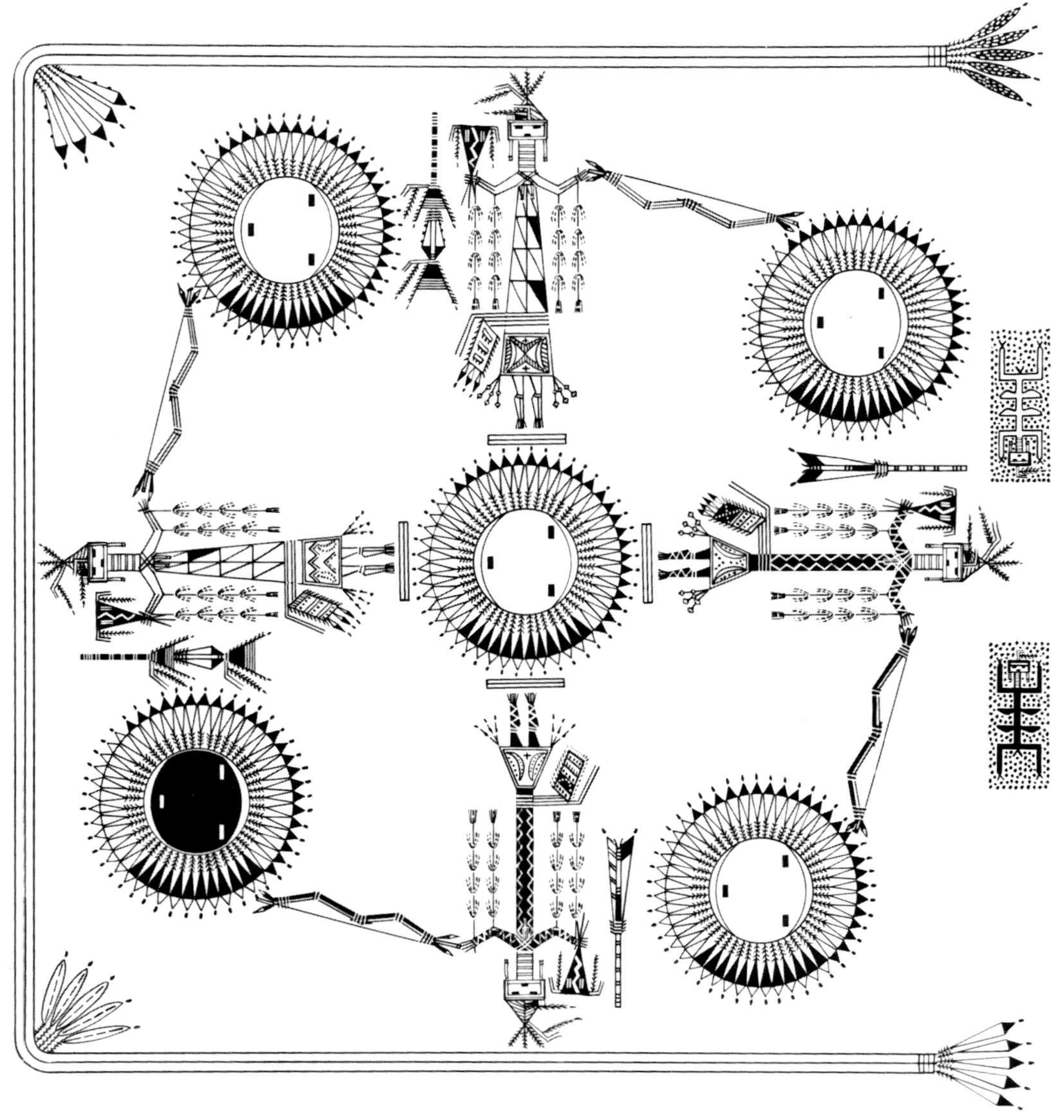

Shooting Chant: Sun Group. "The Whirling Feathers" by Fred Geary. Photograph by Gene Balzer

Drypaintings of overwhelming number, complexity, and significance figure prominently in Navajo ritual. This is not the only tribe in the Native American Southwest, however, to practice this sacred art for purposes of summoning the gods. In fact, sandpainting is widespread throughout the region and has been documented among the Apache and Puebloans in both Arizona and New Mexico, as well as the Papago people of southwestern Arizona. It also existed at one time among tribes on the periphery of the Southwest, such as the Fernandeño, Luiseño, Cupeño, Cahuilla, and Diegueño in southern California and the Cáhita of northern Mexico.

Some southern California tribes used to make geometric and figurative sandpaintings for puberty rites and certain mortuary rituals. We also have accounts from Spanish Jesuits of drypaintings among the Cáhitas of southern Sonora and northern Sinaloa, Mexico, during the sixteenth and seventeenth centuries. These sandpaintings were used in connection with male initiation ceremonies and featured such motifs as plants and animals.

Knowledge of non-Navajo forms of the art is comparatively fragmentary. The factors contributing to this dearth of knowledge include the extinction of sandpainting among some tribes and the widespread practice of excluding all or nearly all outsiders from sandpainting ritual. Puebloans, especially, are notably reluctant to permit the recording and observation of drypainting rites, believing religion's sacred character is best maintained through secrecy. Nevertheless, some examples of non-Navajo drypainting may be briefly described here.

Like the Navajo, the Apache are a Southern Athapaskan people who utilize sandpaintings primarily for curing. The Jicarilla Apaches of northwestern New Mexico make drypaintings depicting the sun, snakes, bear tracks, mountains, rainbows, birds, insects, planets, and divinities in their Holiness Rite, conducted to cure the effects of contact with snakes and bears. The Western Apache in Arizona create "sun disks," easterly oriented drypaintings featuring concentric circles and representations of their versions of Holy People. A patient sits on the painting's center while chanted prayers for recovery are offered. Apache practices of sitting on the painting and applying sand from the painting to parts of the patient's body appear to be closely linked to the ways of their Navajo relations.

Puebloans in Arizona and New Mexico are firmly wedded to the concept of sandpainting. Many scholars believe that they, rather than the Navajo, originated the practice. Their paintings are made inside kivas—subterranean or semi-subterranean ceremonial chambers that evoke mythological emergence from Mother Earth's underworld womb. Typically, a Puebloan drypainting of charcoal, cornmeal, pollens, and mineral pigments is created on the kiva floor. Some Puebloans regard meal-type drypaintings as rainmaking devices and those of the mineral-type as curing aids.

Hopis in northeastern Arizona sometimes arrange a sandpainting over the sipapu, a depression in the kiva's floor connoting the Place of Emergence. These paintings, usually no more than four feet across, are made by workers moving from the outside of the composition inward. A cornmeal line may lead from the drypainting toward the kiva's entryway, either a door or ladder, to guide the spirits who are summoned.

Colors in Puebloan drypaintings are linked to directional symbolism. The specifics of this symbolic system vary, but generally north is represented by either yellow or black; west is signified by blue, green, or yellow; south is indicated by the use of red or blue; white stands for the east; while the zenith and nadir may be either all colors or black. Designs include clouds, rainbows, snakes (because of their relationship to lightning), the sun, moon, and stars, and kachinas (essentially Holy People).

Most drypaintings made by these agricultural people are created to promote rainfall and the fertility of crops. Other reasons for making sandpaintings include hunting magic, curing, and as protection against witchcraft. One difference between Navajo and Puebloan drypainting lies in the Puebloans' primary emphasis on promoting the group good, whereas Navajo practice focuses most intensely on benefiting a particular individual. However, this point of differentation is one of degree. In fact, Navajos attending sandpainting ceremonies do so secure in the knowledge that while the patient is the primary beneficiary of the Holy Peoples' attention, they too receive blessings from the ritual.

The Hopi also use drypaintings in a numerous ceremonies. During the Bean Dance, or Powamu, for example, the initiation of boys and girls into the mainstream of Hopi society takes place. Part of the Bean Dance ritual calls for initiates to stand on a drypainting and receive a ceremonial beating from kachina impersonators wielding yucca whips. One sandpainting design from this ceremony depicts Mother of Kachinas flanked by a pair of Whipper Kachinas. Scattered throughout the painting are dots of various colors that symbolize ripening plants.

While sandpainting still flourishes among Puebloans, albeit behind a closely drawn curtain of secrecy, it is practically moribund among the Papago of southwestern Arizona. Papago drypaintings, like those of the Navajo, alleviate disease-bearing effects of contact with various animals, birds, insects and so on. Among the agents of danger are Wind, Horned Toad, and Owl.

Owl Sickness most often comes from contact with ghosts or too much grieving for a dead person. Injuring or killing a horned toad may cause Horned Toad Sickness, which can manifest itself as rheumatism or swelling of the back and limbs. Wind Sickness, inflicted by a whirlwind, leads to back pains, problems with the legs, or dizziness. Apparently, it is the only one of these ailments for which a daytime ceremony is mandated.

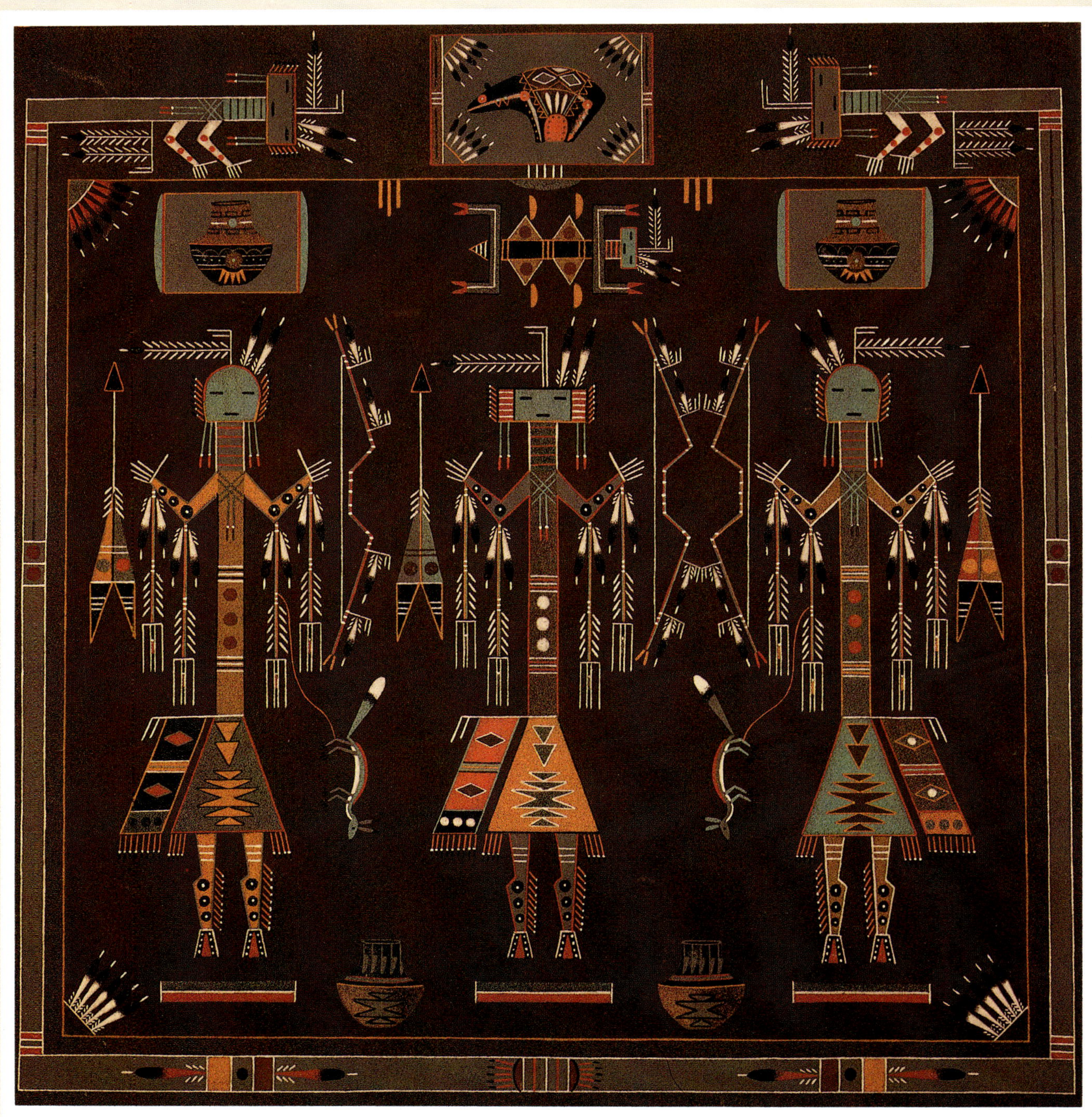

"Atsa Yashi" by George Joe. MNA Gift Shop. Photograph by Gene Balzer

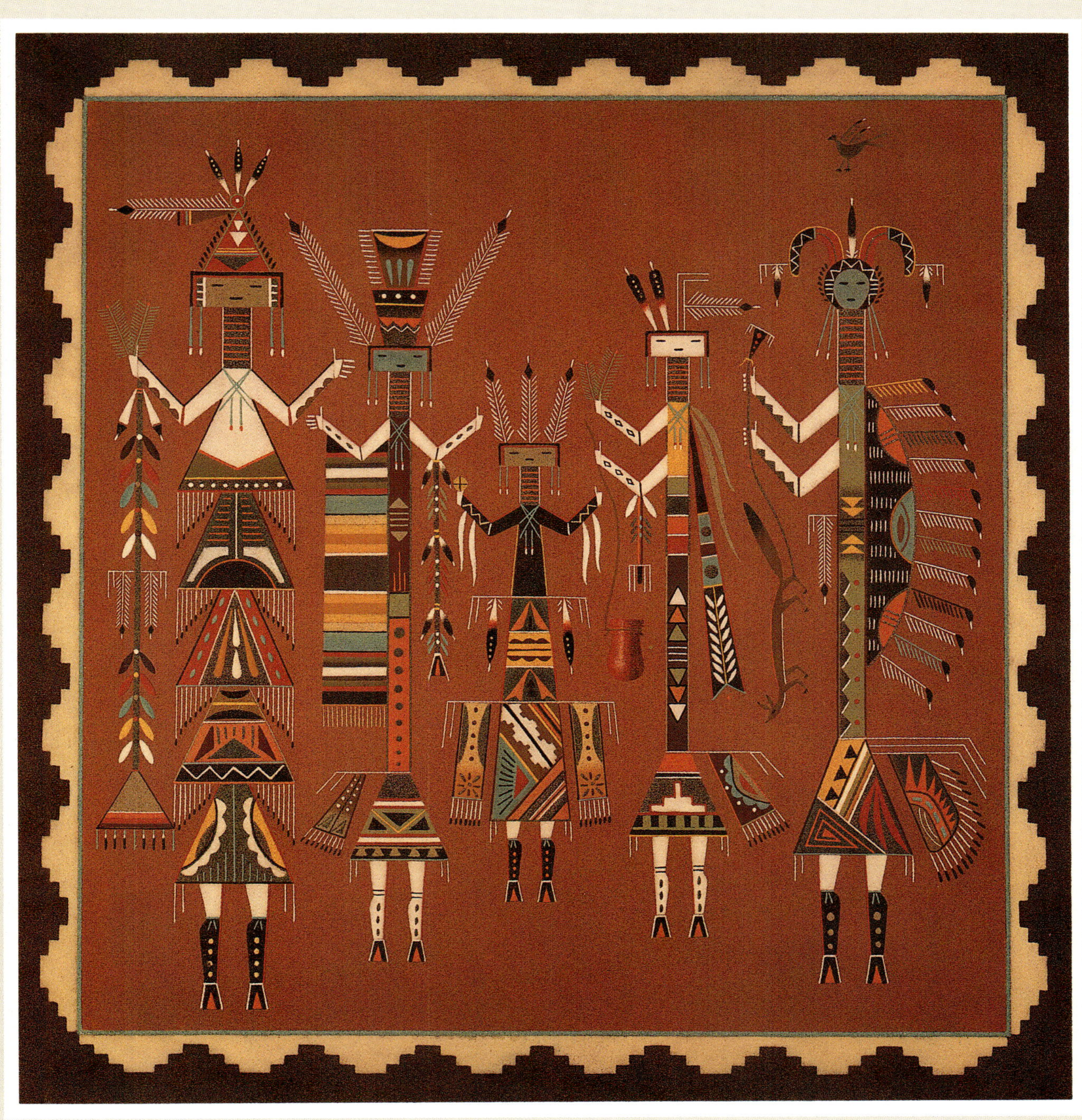

"Yei Bei Chai" by Nelson Lewis. MNA Gift Shop. Photograph by Gene Balzer

Papago sandpaintings are made outdoors and impart blessings not only for the patient but anyone present who suffers from the same complaint. The curer, or medicine man, traces an outline of the sandpainting on the ground which then is filled in by his assistants. As might be expected, the pigments in Papago drypainting embody directional significance also: white from ash for the east; the green of creosote leaves is associated with the south; mesquite charcoal yields a black representing the west; and red rock or lichens signify the north. Designs used in these drypaintings include rectangles, concentric circles, mountain lions, horned toads, deer tracks, birds, bears, and lizards.

We can see that drypainting exists in much of the Native American Southwest. The fact that the sacred art has disappeared from some peripheral points—as among the southern California tribes and the Cáhita of northern Mexico—raises the possibility it previously may have been considerably more widespread than is the case today. In any event, drypainting commonly is associated with summoning the gods for some purpose, whether it be to request increased rainfall, secure Mother Earth's fecundity, or dispel evil forces.

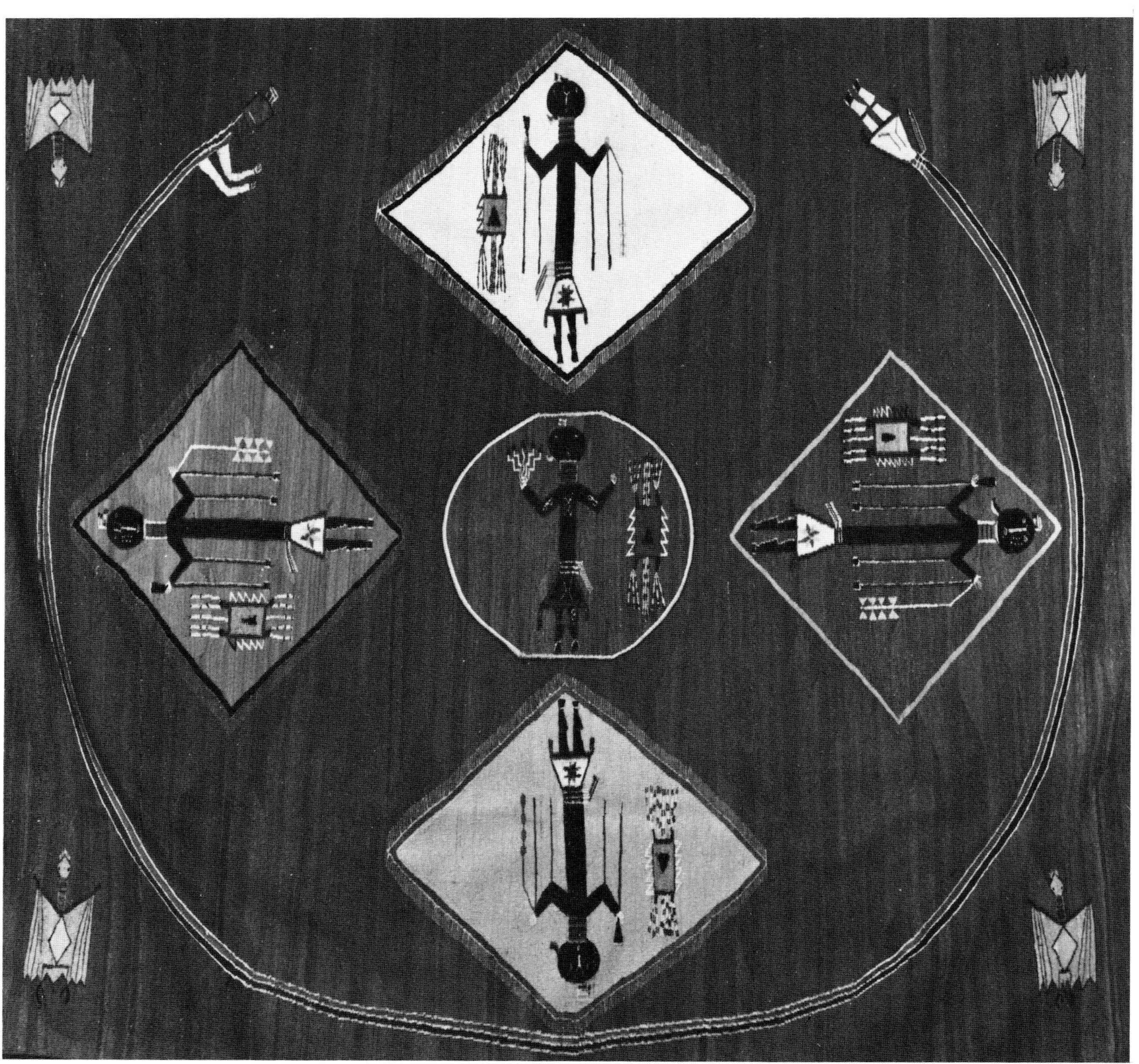

Navajo Klah "Mountain Chant" Sandpainting Rug. Handspun, 83" x 97", Gladwin Collection, 1925-1935. Photograph by Gene Balzer

# Sandpainting Origins

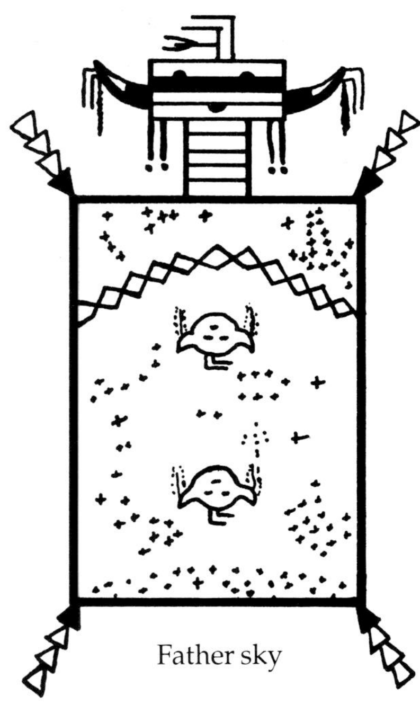

Father sky

Attempting to pinpoint the origin of drypainting in the Native American Southwest is a tempting but not particularly rewarding task. The impermanence of individual sandpaintings prevents comparing one tribe's work, in, say, the mid-16th century, with that of another. This same elusive quality also renders moot questions of whether or not a tribe practiced the sacred art in the remote past and creates questions about sandpaintings' origins that are interesting but ultimately beyond resolution.

We do not know if sandpainting spread from California into the Southwest, which doesn't seem particularly likely, or from Mexico into the Southwest, a circuit more in keeping with the movement of ideas and cultural traits during the region's prehistory. Sandpainting may also have been an independent invention within the prehistoric Southwest.

In any event, drypainting studies have long focused on the Navajo, who possess the most comprehensive and complex inventory of sandpaintings. Few scholars, however, actually believe that Navajos are responsible for drypainting's inception. It seems more likely that they acquired the concept of creating these temporary altars from neighboring Puebloans.

In the wake of the Pueblo Revolt of 1680, an upheaval that drove the Spanish from New Mexico for twelve years, Navajo-Puebloan contact became extensive. This especially was the case between the 1690s and 1770s, when many Puebloans desired total escape from Spanish domination after the Spanish reconquest of New Mexico in 1692. There seems to have been considerable intermarriage during this phase of Navajo and Puebloan history. Such Navajo practices as weaving and reckoning descent through the female line, for example, strike some scholars as evidence of Puebloan influence. The same is true of drypainting.

Frank Hamilton Cushing, a pioneering anthropologist who began his work among the Zuñis in the 1870s, suggested that sandpainting evolved from paintings on kiva walls. Today's kiva paintings, made in connection with nonpublic rituals, are washed away at the conclusion of a ceremony. In former times, these mythological scenes and symbolic prayer designs were plastered over. We know this because some prehistoric kiva murals have survived, notably those at the abandoned settlements at Kuau-a and Pottery Mound in New Mexico and the crumbled Hopi villages of Awatovi and Kawaika-a in Arizona.

Several features associated with prehistoric

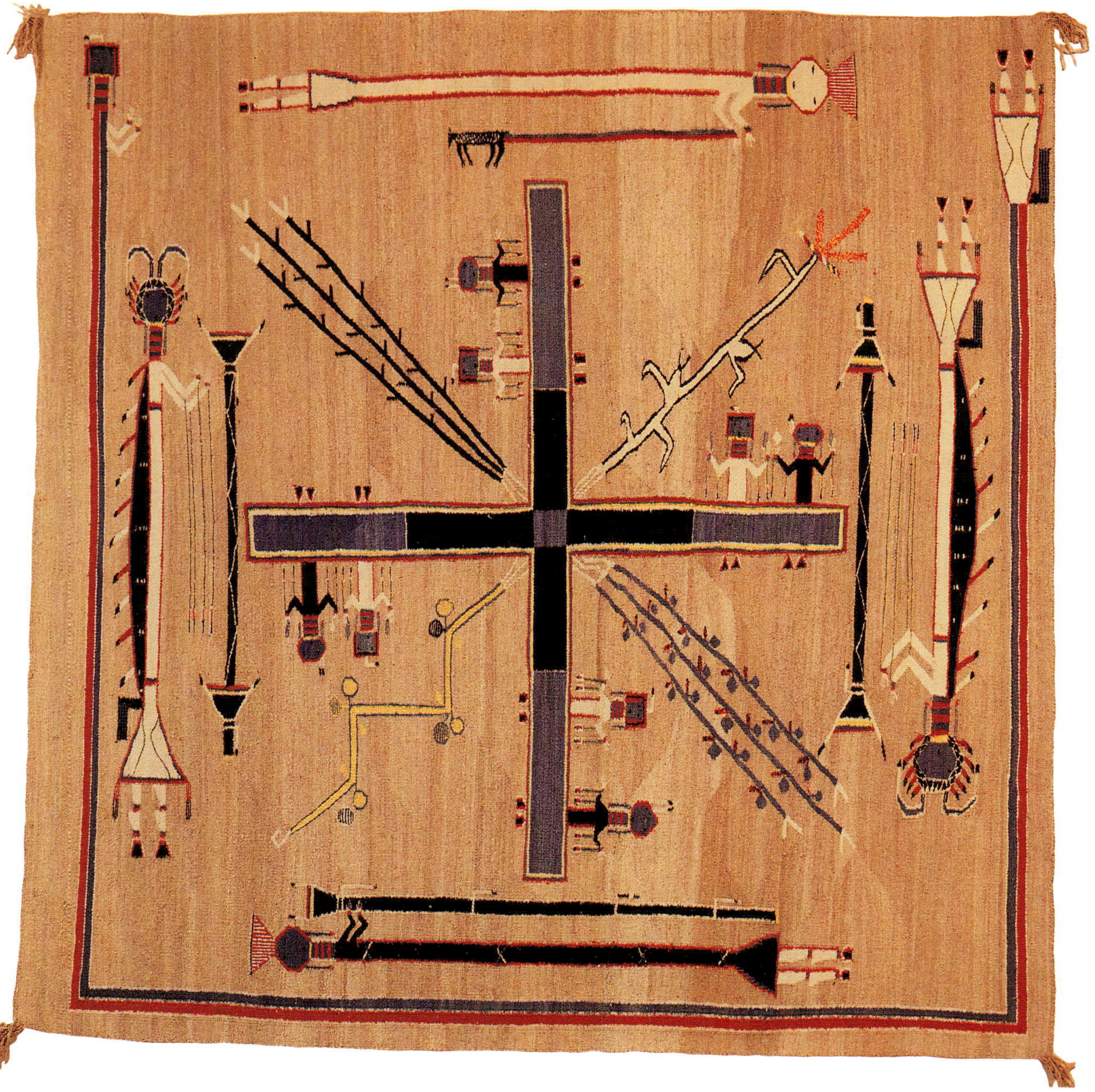

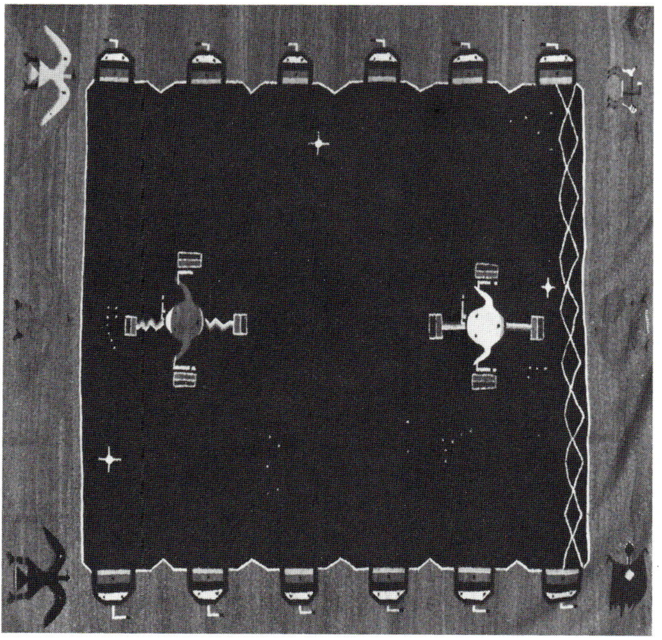

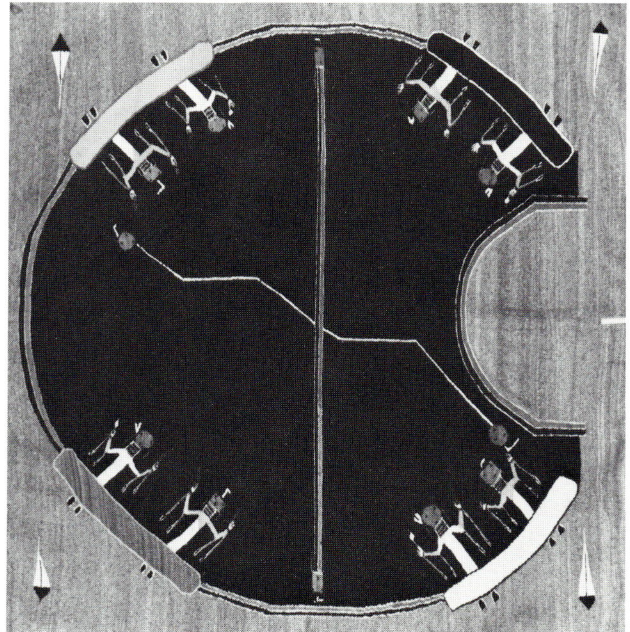

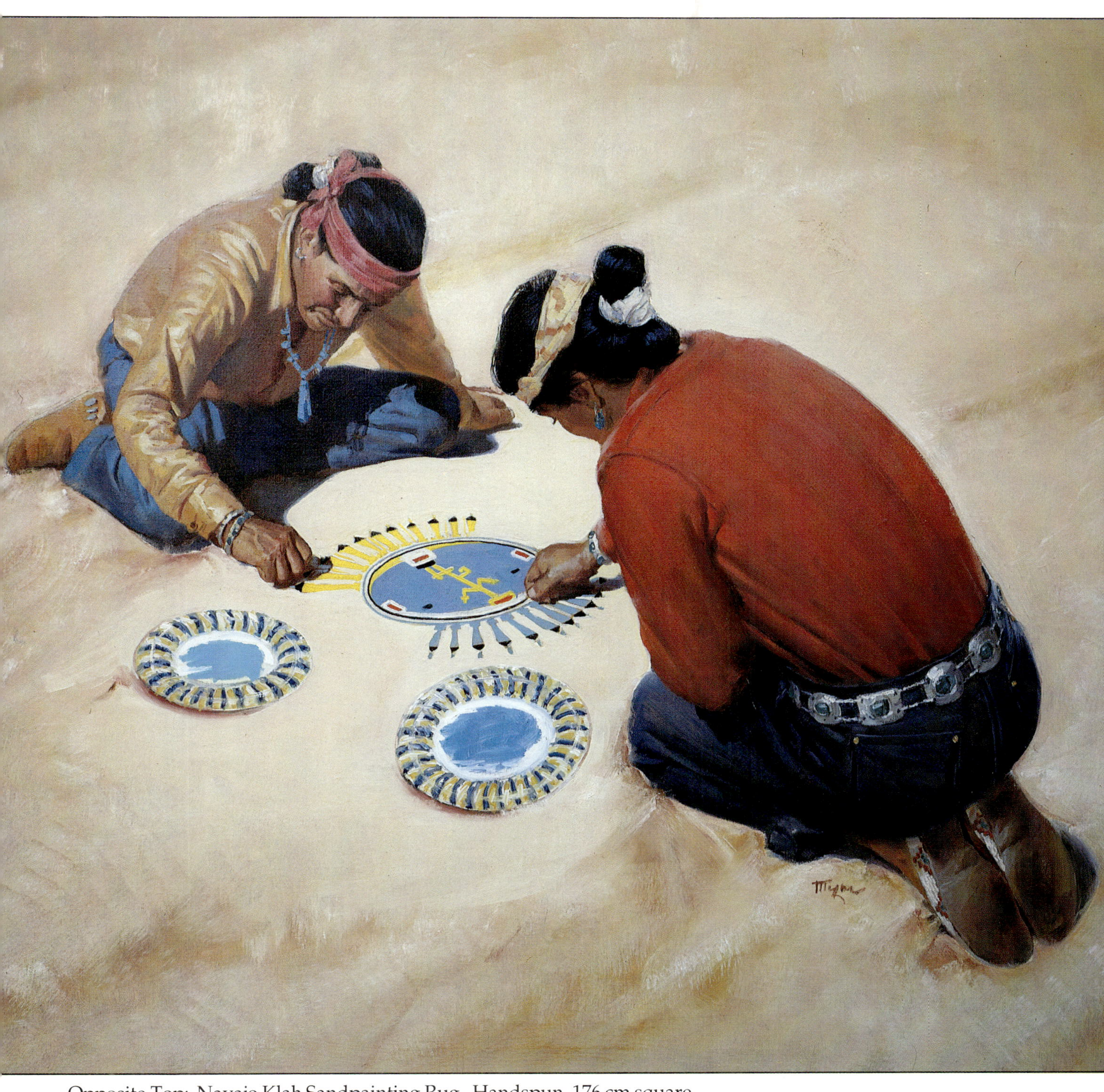

Opposite,Top: Navajo Klah Sandpainting Rug. Handspun, 176 cm square,
Made by Gladys Manuelito (Klah's niece), Gladwin Collection, 1925-1935.
Photograph by Gene Balzer
Opposite, Bottom, Left: Navajo Klah Night Sky Sandpainting Rug from Hailway.
Handspun, 66 1/2" x 66 1/2", Gladwin Collection, 1920-1930. Photograph by Gene Balzer
Opposite, Bottom, Right: Navajo Klah Nightway Chant Sandpainting Rug.
Handspun, 62" x 65", Gladwin Collection, 1920-1930. Photograph by Gene Balzer
Above: "Navajo Sandpainters," 33" x 38" painting. Santa Fe Collection of Southwestern Art.
Painter Federic Kimball Mizer.

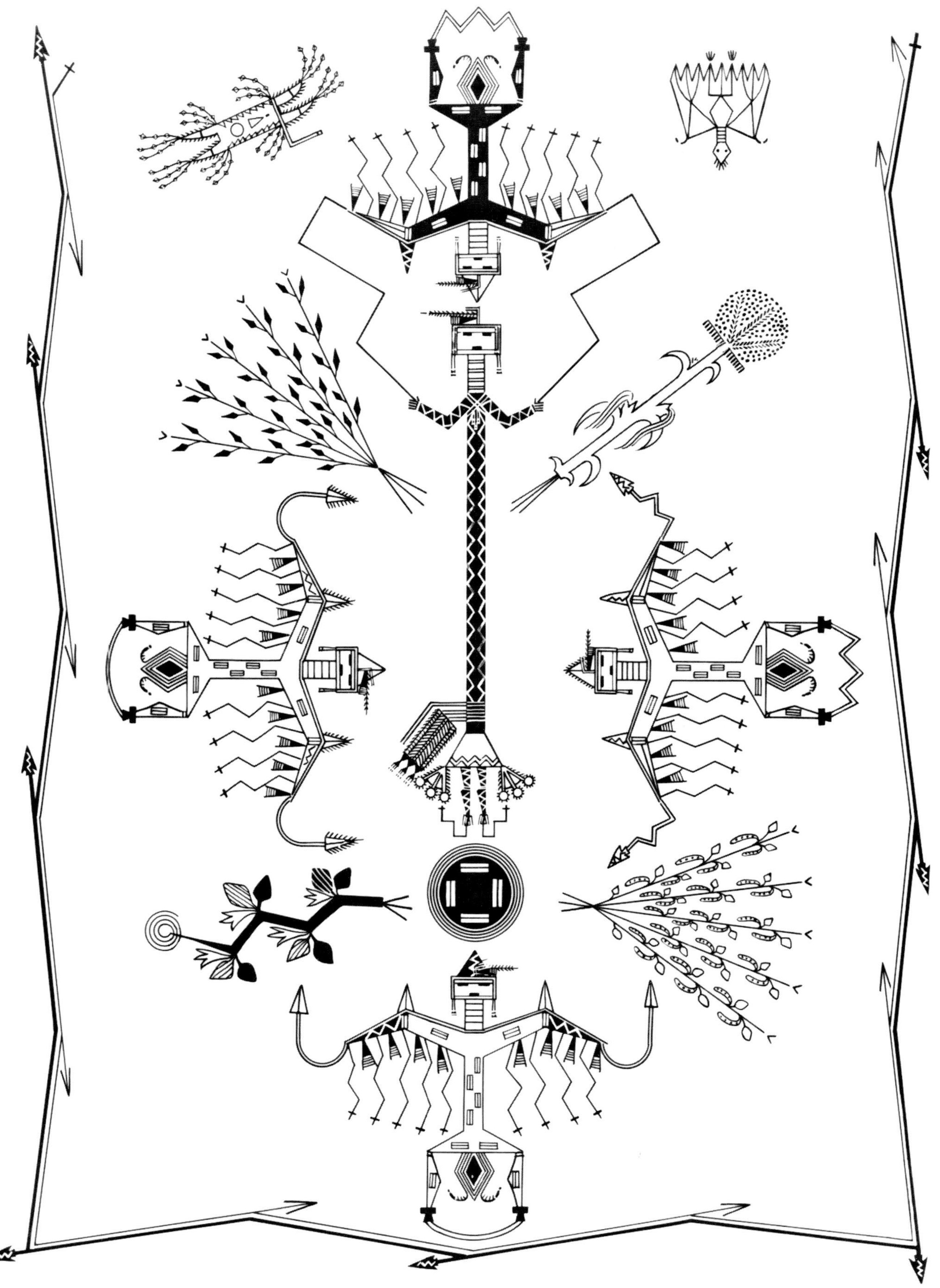

''Holy Man Captured by Thunders'' by Fred Geary. Photograph by Gene Balzer

kiva murals are seen in Navajo drypainting. In both cases, paintings are obliterated after fulfilling their purpose. In many instances, kiva paintings display clearly defined borders possibly setting aside what Hopis call the "kachinas' house"—a term applied to sacred places and the boundary designs on their own sandpaintings. This border delineates sacred space and separates the sacred from the profane in much the same way as do the Navajo guardian lines or garlands.

Additional clues link prehistoric kiva murals and Navajo drypainting. The former, for example, depict supernaturals, or men impersonating divinities, wearing kilts; kilts also are worn by Holy People in Navajo sandpaintings. The motif of corn growing from a cloud terrace with the plant surmounted by a bird is found in both kiva paintings and Navajo sandpaintings. The conical caps of the Hopis' Twin War Gods—counterparts of Monster Slayer and Born for Water—appear in Navajo drypaintings. The headdresses of upright feathers on figures in kiva murals are akin to those worn by the Navajos' Talking God and Calling God.

One anthropomorphic figure appearing on a kiva wall at Jeddito displays a black face with white circular eyes and mouth, a white line zigzagging diagonally across his face, and his forehead is decorated with a white crescent and seven white dots. He resembles various Hopi kachinas, including Pókoma (Dog), Hoho Mana (Zuni Maiden), and Sio Avách´hoya (Zuni Corn), as well as Mástop (Death Fly), whose dark face is decorated with white-dot representations of the Dipper and Pleiades constellations. In addition, the Awatovi figure's visage is strikingly reminiscent of Hastsezini, or Black God, a Ye'i on whose face the Pleiades also appear.

Yet Navajo sandpaintings and Puebloan kiva murals are stylistically different. Humans and anthropomorphic figures in kiva paintings are blocky in form while those in Navajo sandpaintings display a linear, streamlined appearance more akin to the rock art created by the Fremont Culture of eastern Utah and western Colorado between A. D. 950 and 1200.

Certainly the form taken by many of the figures in Navajo sandpaintings was established quite some time ago. Rock art in the Dinetah region that dates to the late sixteenth and early seventeenth centuries—the time when Puebloan influence on the tribe is believed to have been most intense—includes readily identifiable forms of the Hero Twins and a number of Ye'i, including Humpback with his pack of seeds and mist, Fringed Mouth, the Female God, and perhaps Red God, Talking God, and Calling God as well.

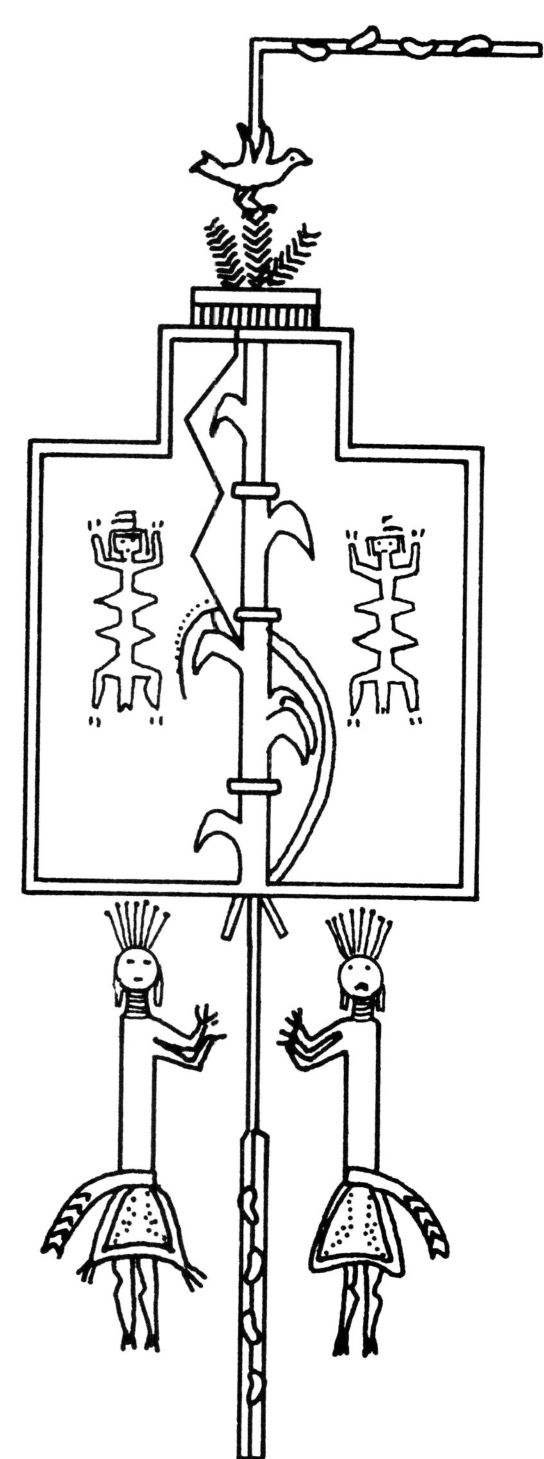

The path of life is shown as a cornstalk crossing a white field. The lower two figures are the Ethkay-nah-ashi, the transmitters of life, and the upper figures are Dontso, the messenger fly.

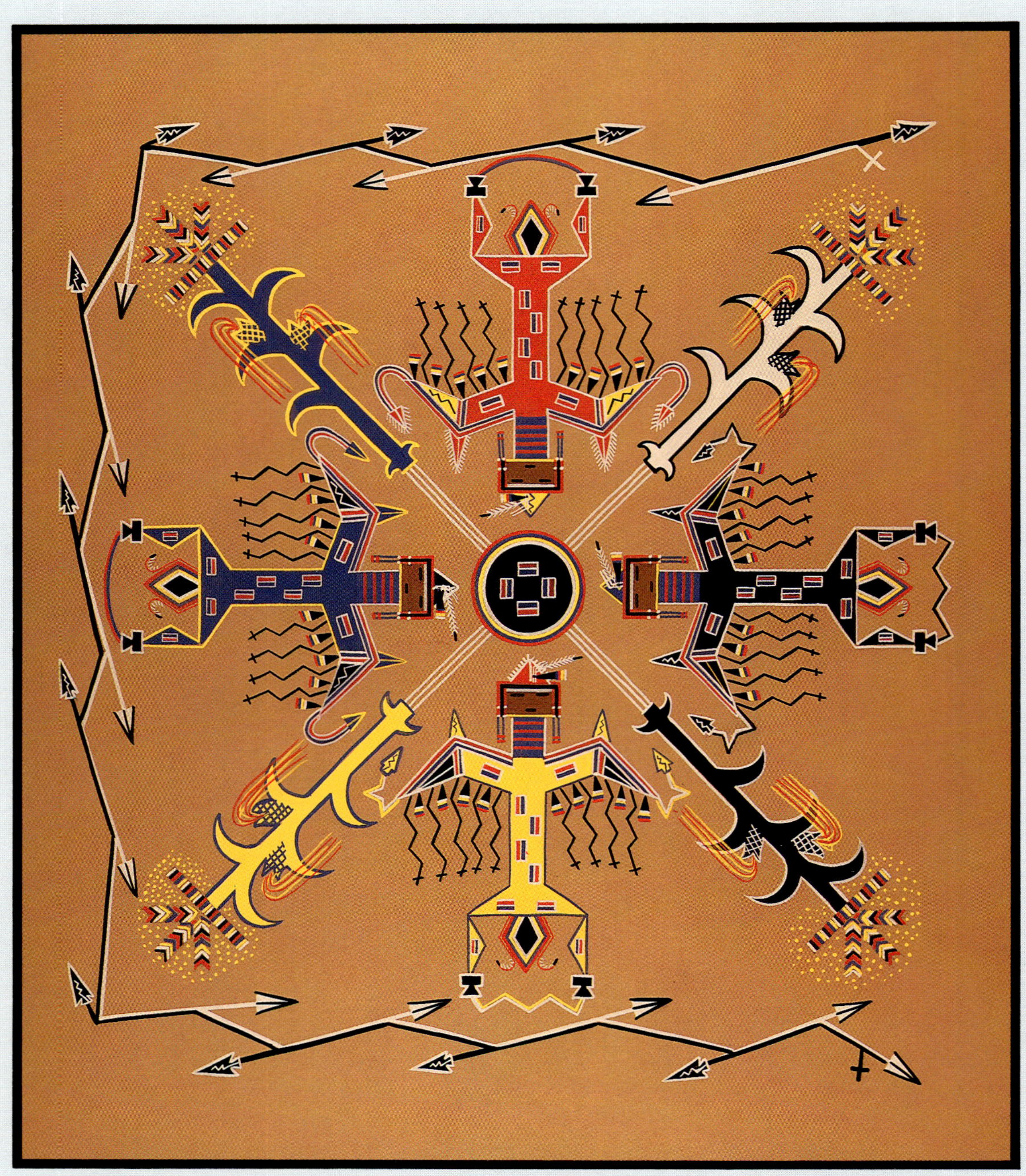

Shooting Chant: Thunder Gods. ''The Home of the Thunder Gods'' by Hosteen Bezody. Photograph by Gene Balzer

# Stability and Change in Drypainting

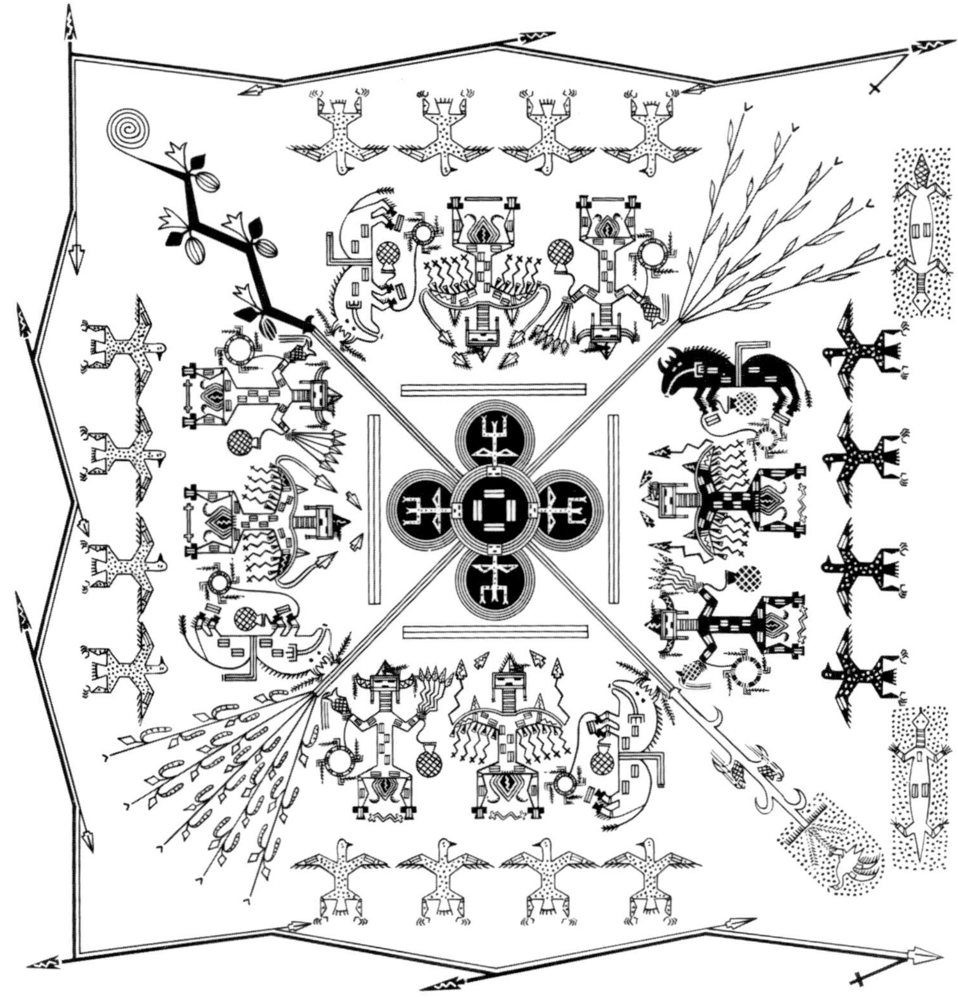

"The Water People" by Fred Geary. Photograph by Gene Balzer

Among the Navajo, no Singer ever conveys all of his sacred knowledge to an apprentice. Instead, the novice seeks the missing pieces of information from another medicine man. When those missing pieces are not applied to fitting the puzzle together, for whatever reason, a ritual may actually disappear. In ceremonies passed along by oral tradition there naturally is a certain amount of variety in ritual; no two performances can ever be truly identical. Yet as an art form, Navajo drypainting has proved remarkably consistent.

Judging by drawings of sandpaintings made as early as 1884 by Washington Matthews, a physician who worked for the U.S. Army at Fort Wingate, New Mexico, this sacred art displays impressive stability. Changes do occur, to be sure. The greatest variation in sandpaintings is seen in the designs placed on Holy People's kilts and pouches, for which a painter apparently is given virtually free rein. Horses, which could hardly have been seen by Navajos prior to Francisco Vásquez de Coronado's expedition into the Southwest in 1540, have been introduced somewhere along the line into sandpaintings. But the overall form and points of detail have displayed remarkable consistency for at least the past century or so.

This is because drypainting is a sacred prescription akin to a chemical formula. Water results from the marriage of two parts hydrogen and one part oxygen. Should that formula be

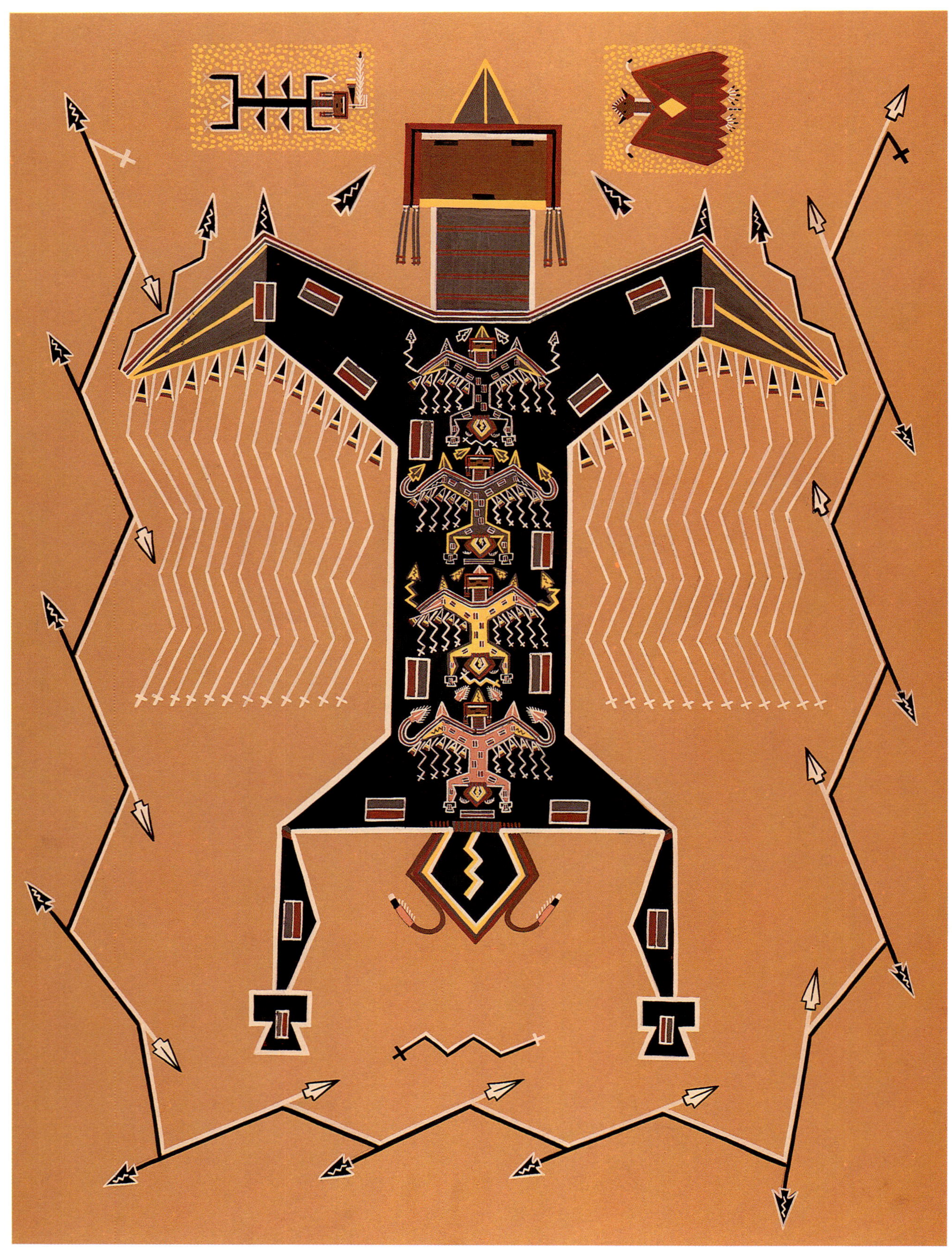

Shooting Chant: The Big Thunder (Thunder God) Y-ne tso
"Thunder Huge" by Fred Geary. Photograph by Gene Balzer

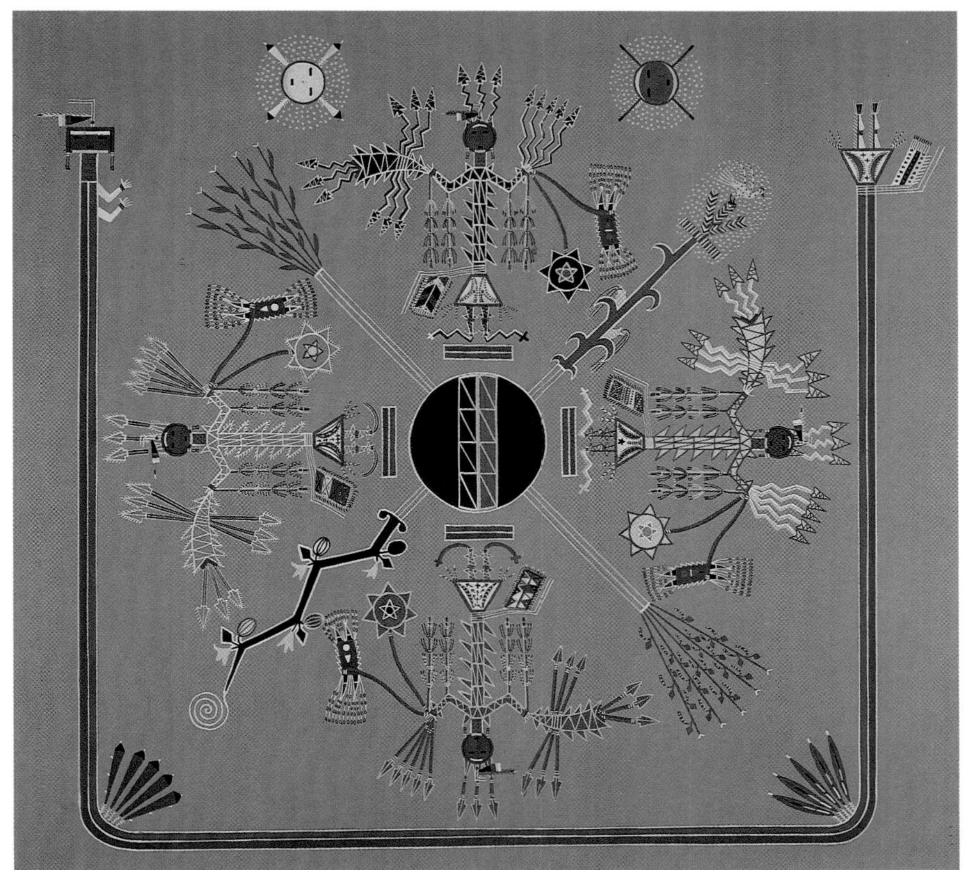

Top: Shooting Chant: Group Naye-nez-rani. "The House of Many Points" by Fred Geary. Photograph by Gene Balzer
Bottom: Beadway: Snakes lift scavenger through the sky hole. "The Second and Final Ascension of VA-HOO-DE-DAHE" by Fred Geary. Photograph by Gene Balzer

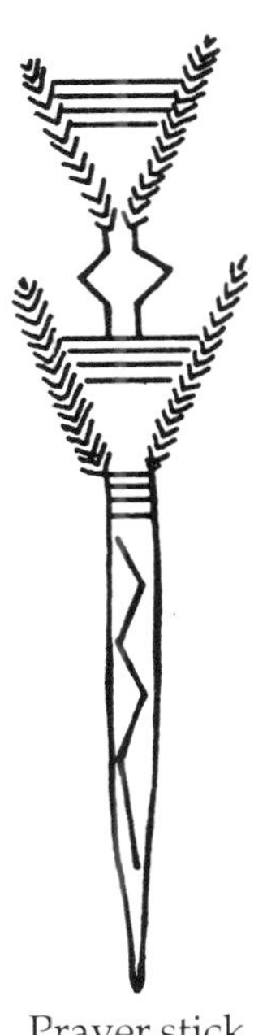

Prayer stick

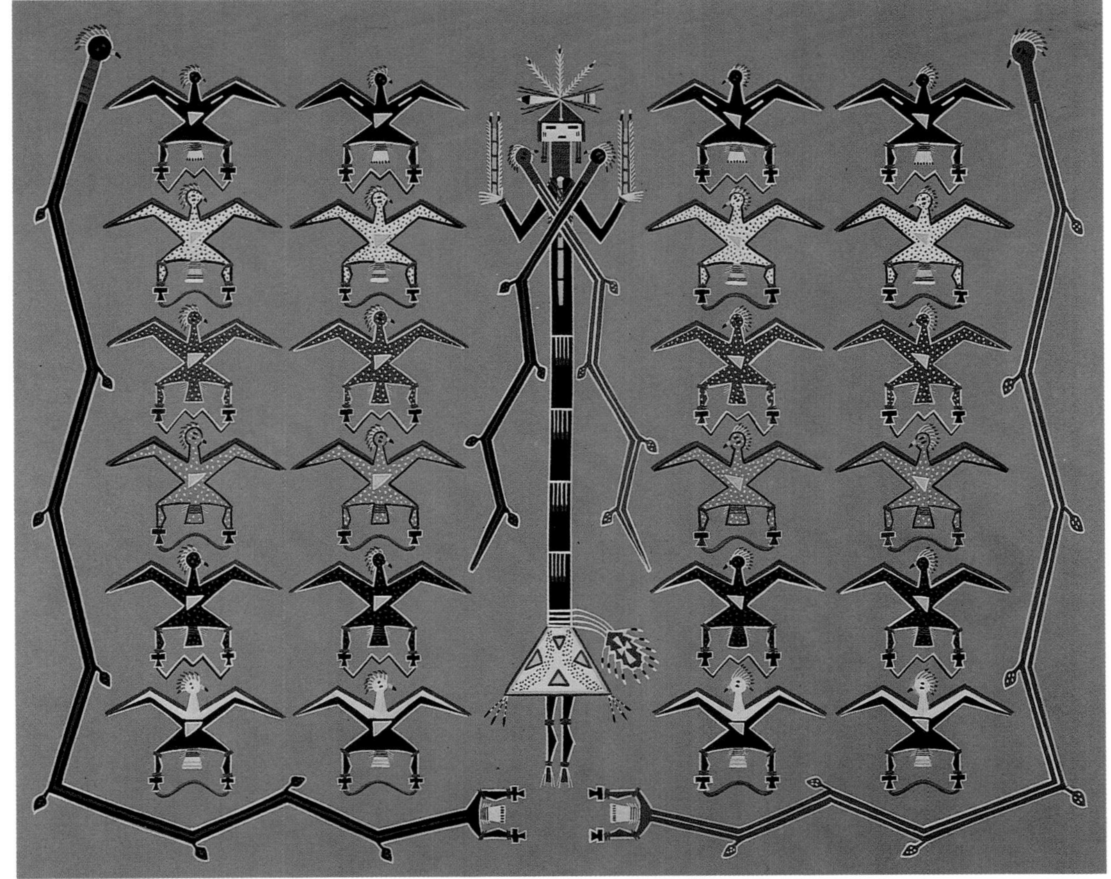

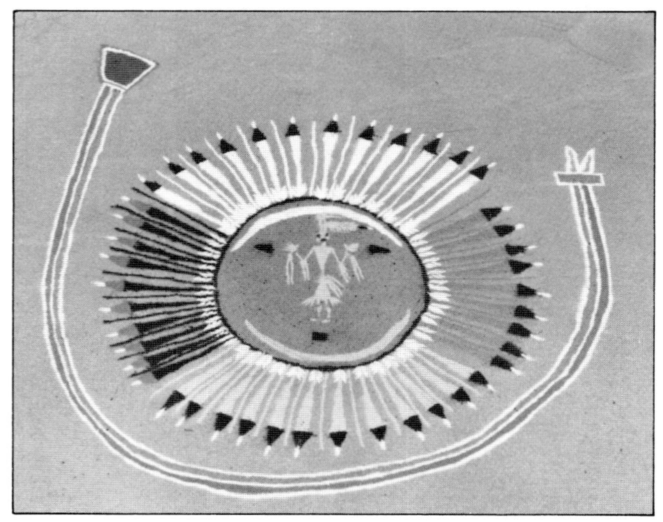

changed, the result, whatever it might be, cannot possibly be water. A Navajo medicine man who alters a sandpainting undermines the purpose of a curing ceremony, for the gods cannot be summoned by other than the means they themselves established for accomplishing that holy mission. There exists no compelling reason for a Singer to alter the artistic formula of something he knows works. When, for example, was the last time a priest amended the Lord's Prayer or a rabbi inserted his own lines into the Kaddish?

There is one obvious cause for deviation, however. Anyone creating a permanent version of a sandpainting would be well-advised to render the work's power impotent by deliberate alteration. This happens in the case of tapestries and drawings that depict drypainting designs, as well as in the permanent sandpainting images that fill shops and galleries throughout the Southwest.

Preservation of sandpaintings runs counter to this sacred art's purpose. Yet drawings of sandpaintings have been made since Washington Matthews started sketching them in the 1880s. He did so despite strenuous objections from Navajos, who feared evil would befall anyone in possession of what amounted to a never-ending cry beseeching the Holy People's appearance.

However, within a few years, even some Navajos began making records of sandpaintings. The two most influential of these preservers of arcane knowledge were Lefthanded (c. 1867-1937), widely known as Hosteen Klah, and Miguelito (c. 1865-1936), also called Red Point. Significantly, each was a medicine man, and both probably altered their depictions of sandpaintings in ways that rendered the powerful and dangerous formulae for summoning the gods inoperable.

Lefthanded was a practitioner of various chantways: Nightway, Shootingway, and Hailway, among others. He is noted for weaving large, richly detailed, and pleasingly colored reproductions of sandpainting designs. Although weaving is women's work among Navajos, Lefthanded was thought of as "transformed," a condition commonly believed to have resulted either through hermaphroditism at birth or castration by Ute enemies as a child. Lefthanded's first sandpainting textile, a rendering of the "Whirling Logs" design seen in Nightway, probably was woven in 1919.

Over an eighteen-year period, Lefthanded

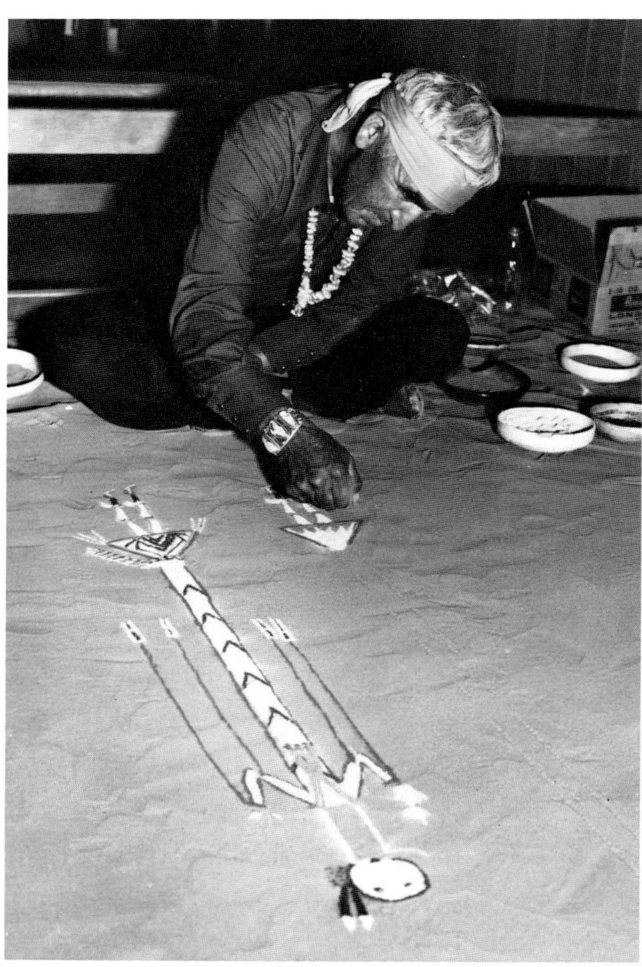

Top, Left: "Chiricahua Windway; Pollen Boy on the Sun," Sandpainting demonstration display at the Navajo Craftsman Show 1970.
Photograph from MNA collections
Above: Lon Kerley demonstrating sandpainting at the Navajo Craftsman Show 1976.
Photograph from MNA collections

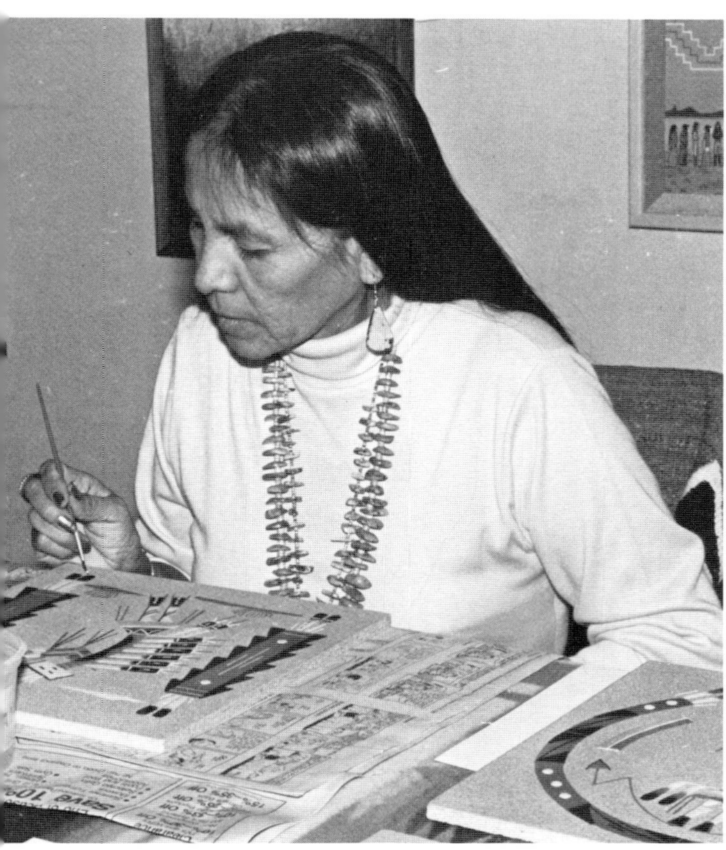

Above: Navajo sandpainting demonstrator at 1987 Navajo Craftsman Show. Photograph by Robyn Jones
Below: Sandpainting demonstration display at the Navajo Craftsman Show 1971.
Photograph from MNA collections

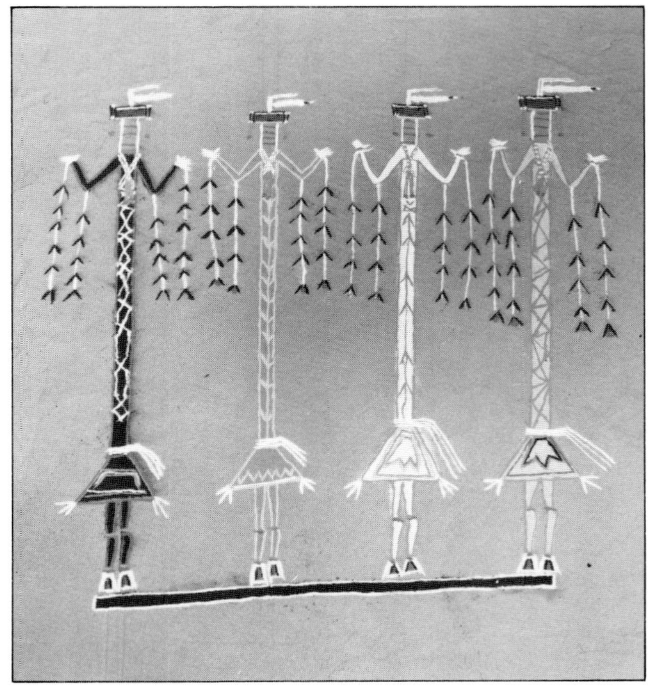

and two of his nieces created no fewer than seventy drypainting tapestries. Lefthanded was the sole creator of something less than a quarter of this impressive body of work. During the weaving process, he performed precautionary ceremonies designed to protect his nieces from any adverse effects stemming from working too close to the world of the supernatural.

Numerous reproductions of sandpaintings, painted on paper rather than woven with spun wool, constitute the legacy of Miguelito, one of Lefthanded's contemporaries and a Singer versed in such rituals as Blessingway, Flintway, and Shootingway. Miguelito was an invaluable source for two books that are richly illustrated with depictions of Navajo drypaintings: *Sandpaintings of the Navajo Shooting Chant* by Franc J. Newcomb and Gladys A. Reichard, which appeared in 1937, and Reichard's *Navajo Medicine Man*, published two years later.

Most observers believe that both Miguelito and Lefthanded slightly altered their reproductions of sandpaintings—if only in small ways, through color substitution and the omission or addition of figures. In this way, the reproductions could not be expected to function as true sandpaintings. Edward Sapir, a noted American anthropologist, once recalled that a Navajo sandpainting blanket he purchased in 1929 contained no less than thirty-four such "errors."

Since the 1960s, many Navajos have found a source of income in the virtual mass-production of "sandpaintings." These artisans rely on techniques developed in the 1930s in Gallup, New Mexico, by E. George de Ville and Mae Allendale, a husband-and-wife team of Anglo signpainters. The basic process involves coating wallboard or particle board with glue and applying one or more layers of colored sand in an image-creating pattern; an artist's fixative lightly sprayed over the surface makes the work permanent. The types of images depicted in this way range from altered forms of entire sandpaintings to individual elements seen in drypaintings, to pictures of birds, animals, bucking broncos, and landscapes.

Although technically these depictions are sandpaintings, they are entirely secular in nature. These bits of trading post and curio shop merchandise do not actually duplicate the complex world of symbols seen in southwestern drypainting and neither profane existing religion nor summon the gods.

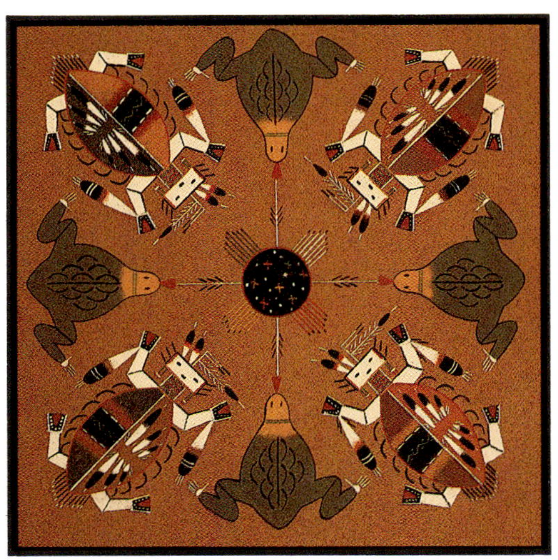

# Southwestern Sandpainting

Summoning the gods with sandpaintings is intriguing, both as a religious act and as a sacred art of the Native American Southwest. The practice of creating what are in effect altars with sand, ground minerals, pulverized flower petals, and the pollen of life-bearing plants has been reported among the Puebloans, Papago, and Apache tribes as well as, most extensively, the Navajos of the the Four Corners region.

How, when, where, and why sandpainting came into existence are questions the impermanent nature of the art must forever conceal. Many interesting questions—such as whether the Navajos acquired the art of drypainting from their Puebloan neighbors—await further investigation. While not all the questions we pose will receive answers, that we are confronted with an ancient practice seems certain.

Many Navajos understandably are sensitive to anthropologists and historians who marshal evidence for the origin of religious practices that runs counter to tribal beliefs. Yet Navajos are not the only people whose accounts on matters spiritual are not necessarily suppported by scholarly discourse. Still, this fact remains. Whether the Navajo obtained knowledge of drypainting from the Holy People or from inspiration triggered by paintings on kiva walls really makes little difference. For what the Navajos have done with sandpainting required their own special genius. It is the Navajo, after all, who carried the art of drypainting in the Native American Southwest to its zenith, achieving an apotheosis of symbolic language by summoning the gods with an utterly grand, unsurpassingly beautiful vision.

In fact, queries and speculation perhaps should not loom as significantly in our consciousness as the profound recognition that sandpainting is not merely a thing of the past but an ongoing feature of life in the Native American Southwest. After all, the gods are still being summoned.

There is something wondrous and comforting in knowing that for countless preceding generations the nightime silence of the high desert has been broken by the the evocative chant of medicine men directing drypainters. Indeed, today's sandpainters of the Navajos' Nightway continue to sing a song recorded more than a century ago:

> In beauty happily I walk.
> With beauty before me I walk.
> With beauty behind me I walk.
> With beauty below me I walk.
> With beauty above me I walk.
> With beauty all around me I walk.
> It is finished again in beauty.
> It is finished in beauty.
> (Washington Matthews *The Night Chant*, 1902)

So it has been for generations without number and so may it be for many years to come. And may the summoning of the gods continue in the ways of the past—conceived and born in beauty.

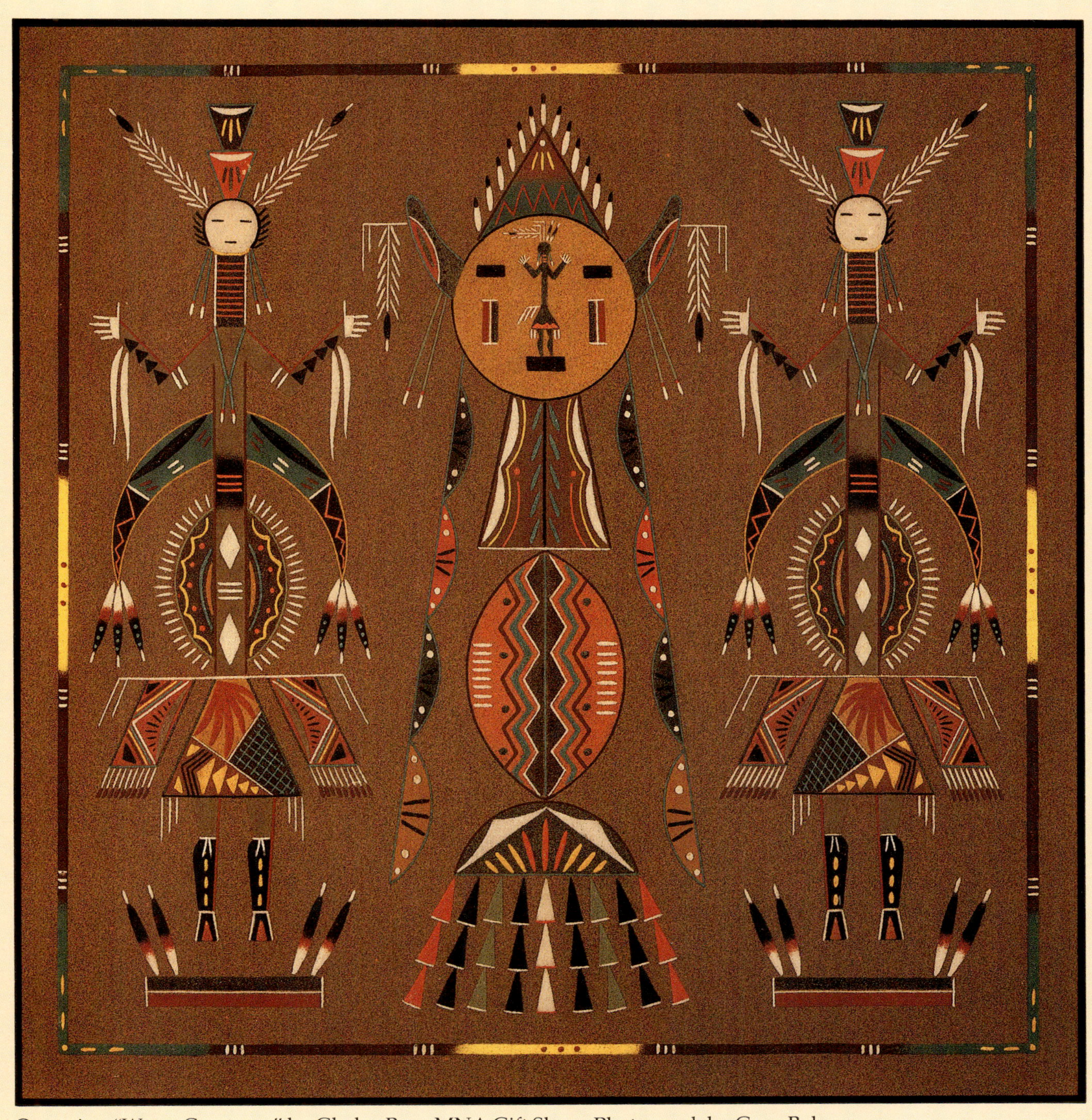

Opposite: "Water Creatures" by Gladys Ben. MNA Gift Shop. Photograph by Gene Balzer
Above: "Sun Verse and Nei Bi Chai" by Nelson Lewis. MNA Gift Shop. Photograph by Gene Balzer

## ACKNOWLEDGMENTS

Anyone writing about drypainting in the Native American Southwest must tender an expression of gratitude to the first of the great researchers in the field, Dr. Washington Matthews. Since his time, other individuals have attained prominence in drypainting studies. These include Gladys Reichard, Franc Newcomb, and Berard Haile, O.F.M., all of whom, sadly, have joined their own gods. Karl Luckert and Leland Wyman have greatly expanded our knowledge of Navajo ceremonialism. To all of these scholars, the author offers his appreciation and respect. Thanks is also due Dorothy House of the Museum of Northern Arizona, who made the Goldwater, Reichard, Euler, and Harvey collections as well as the Wyman Drypainting File available.

## SUGGESTED READING

The body of literature about sandpainting is both rich and abundant. The works listed below constitute a sampling of some of the most informative sources.

Karl W. Luckert
1979 *Coyoteway: A Navajo Holyway Healing Ceremony* (Tucson and Flagstaff: University of Arizona Press and Museum of Northern Arizona Press). Examination of a seldom-performed Navajo ritual, augmented by magnificent on-site photographs.

Washington Matthews
1902 *The Night Chant: A Navaho Ceremony.* (Memoirs of the American Museum of Natural History, Vol. 6).

Washington Matthews
1907 "Navaho Myths, Prayers and Songs," with text and translations. (University of California Publications in American Archaeology and Ethnology, Vol. 5).

Franc Johnson Newcomb
1964 *Hosteen Klah* (Norman: University of Oklahoma Press). The story of Navajo medicine man-weaver Lefthanded, told by a woman noted for her numerous copies of drypaintings.

Franc Johnson Newcomb and Gladys A. Reichard
1937 *Sandpaintings of the Navajo Shooting Chant* (New York: J.J. Augustin) (reprinted, New York: Dover, 1975). Superbly illustrated with copies of Miguelito's Shootingway drawings.

Nancy Parezo
1980 *Navajo Sandpainting: From Religious Act to Commercial Art* (Tucson: University of Arizona Press). Fascinating study of the development of sandpainting as a commercial art.

Gladys A. Reichard
1939 *Navajo Medicine Man* (New York: J.J. Augustin) (Reprinted as *Navajo Medicine Man Sandpaintings,* New York: Dover, 1977). Copies of Miguelito's sandpainting facsimiles from Beadway and Shootingway.

Donald Sandner
1979 *Navaho Symbols of Healing* (New York: Harcourt Brace Jovanovich). Intriguing analysis by a clinical psychiatrist of Navajo practices for curing physical and mental ills.

Leland C. Wyman
1983 *Southwest Indian Drypainting* (Santa Fe and Albuquerque: School of American Research and University of New Mexico Press). Perhaps the finest source to consult in becoming acquainted with sandpainting. A distillation of the knowledge acquired by a giant in the field.

Leland C. Wyman
1970 *Blessingway* (Tucson: University of Arizona Press). Wyman began writing about Navajo culture more than fifty years ago, and the depth of his scholarship is displayed in this fine volume.

## ABOUT THE AUTHOR

Ronald McCoy holds a Ph.D. in history and an M.A. in anthropology. He has written extensively about the Indian tribes of the American West and is a recipient of the Wrangler Award for publishing excellence from the National Cowboy Hall of Fame and Western Heritage Center. His "Circles of Power," a 1984 issue of *Plateau* about American Indian shields of the Southwest and Great Plains, won the American Association of Museums' Award of Distinction. Dr. McCoy long associated with the Paul Dyck Foundation-Research Institution of American Indian Culture, teaches history at Emporia State University in Emporia, Kansas.

## A NOTE ON THE MIGUELITO SANDPAINTINGS

Fred Geary, artist for the Fred Harvey Company, painted these illustrations from originals by Miguelito in the John Frederick Huckel Collection. The Geary paintings were part of the bequest of Katherine Harvey to the Museum of Northern Arizona.

Line drawings by Lloyd Moylan were taken from *A Study of Navajo Symbolism* by Newcomb, Fishler and Wheelwright. Peabody Museum, 1956.

Printing by Land O' Sun
*Plateau* Managing Editor: Diana Clark Lubick
Graphic Design by Dianne Moen Zahnle
Typography by Mac Type Net